By Ferne Carter Chapman

DEDICATION

Dedicated to my parents, my late husband, and to our children Lynne Chapman Gibbs and her husband Larry, Jack and Karen Chapman and their children Brandon and Breanna.

—Ferne

Town & Country Creative Breads

Published by JacLynn Publishing, 4007 North Whitman, Tacoma, WA 98407
Printed by Graphic Press, Tacoma
Art work by Madeline Jones and Julius Zimmerman
Cover Design: McGowan Advertising, Linda K. Bachand,
   Creative Director/Designer
Photography by Clemente
Forward by Patrick M. Donovan, N.D.
Edited by Karl G. Schlosser, M.P.W.

ACKNOWLEDGMENTS

Mildred Hoffman, Darcea Schiesl, Linda Mahalic, Marian & William Holmes, Jr., and everyone who helped make this book possible.

All quotations used with permission of their respective authors.

RESOURCES:

Dottie's Bosch Kitchen
1st & Main Street
Puyallup, WA

Lakewood Natural Foods
100th & Bridgeport Way, S.W.
Tacoma, WA

Westgate Nutrition Shop
26th & Pearl Street
Tacoma, WA

ISBN 0-9637312-9-7
Library of Congress Catolog Card Number 93-80029

Note from the editor: Because of space limitations, the author has chosen to typeset ingredients in two-columns. The word ''Tablespoon'' will always be CAPITALIZED to distinguish it from ''teaspoon.'' Measurements are spelled out (''ounces'' rather than ''oz'') for clarity. For those readers with food allergies or sensitivities, please feel free to modify the recipes as desired. Baking is a creative process, after all.

Printed in the United States of America on Recycled Paper.

FOREWORD

by Patrick M. Donovan, N.D.

Throughout human evolution, diet has been a major factor influencing the formation and development of our bodies and genetic makeup. Our present physiology and biochemical nature is a result and reflection of our traditional dietary patterns as well as our environment. Programmed by a diet rich in fiber, complex carbohydrates and micro-nutrients from un-processed, whole foods, our physiology has been dependent on such a diet to maintain its optimal performance and function. In other words, "we are what we eat." And "we must eat well to be well."

Ferne has done us all a wonderful service by writing this book. She has provided us with a delightful, adventurous and, certainly, sensually rewarding way to "eat well." And, therefore, "be well." Her bread recipes bring together the best of two worlds. They provide a rich source of the fiber, complex carbohydrates and micro-nutrients needed by our bodies to promote and maintain health while being, at the same time, gustatorially ecstatic creations. (Some more than others, I grant you. But you must find your own favorites.) This is quite an accomplishment, since grains are not inherently gustatorially ecstatic in themselves.

This speaks highly of her skills as a baker. Skills acquired over many years of "foolin' with food." Her experience has given her an old country wisdom about baking that clearly flavors her recipes with "robust heartiness." Her section on general baking information is a clear example of this and imparts many tidbits of country kitchen wisdom. Her section on wheat-free breads demonstrates an awareness of the prominence of wheat allergies in our society and the need for alternatives. Her alternatives do not sacrifice flavor for utility, as some wheat-free recipes do. In short, she has done a good job putting together healthy and delicious bread, muffin and scone recipes that are hearty and adventurous, yet simple.

If, like most people, you need to add more fiber to your diet and improve its overall quality, I couldn't think of many more delicious ways to do it than to add some of Ferne's breads to your daily diet. I hope it's not too forward of me to suggest you experience one of the many high-fiber, gustatory ecstasies awaiting you in this book. But I couldn't resist. It may be one of the only chances you get. After all, there aren't many to be had! Oh, and please, experience it with a friend. It will be more memorable.

PROLOGUE

The Carter Homestead was situated on the open prairie, in the "Flicker Tail" state of North Dakota. The rundown farm was nestled in a cradle formed by sun-baked hills (to the south and west) and a lush green valley with running springs and a quicksand bog (to the north and east). The bog entrapped many unsuspecting animals and, as the story goes, a few Indian inhabitants and early settlers. The quicksand bog was located on the southwest shore of an alkali lake.

Chase Lake (and the old cottonwood tree at its edge) was used as a landmark by anyone giving directions in the county. A choke cherry patch along the south shore of Chase Lake made this area the focal point of our childhood entertainment.

The early history of North Dakota took place on The Great Drift Plain, less than one hundred years before our homestead was acquired under The Homestead Act of 1862. The Lewis and Clark Expedition scouted past our acreage on their way to the Pacific coast. (A statue of "The Bird Woman" Sakagewea is mounted on the state capital grounds at Bismarck, North Dakota.) The Great Plains, according to the United States Geological Survey, is the center of the North American continent. The prairies in our territory supported large herds of buffalo, elk, deer and antelope, all of which furnished food, shelter and clothing for the Indian tribes. Fur trading was an integral part of life among the Indian families; our family engaged in the practice during the Great Depression. In the fall, wildlife attracted hunters to the area.

Our climate was one of alternating dry and wet years, with crops ranging from very good to none. When that occurred, it was dandelion green time for us. We were told by our parents that "dandelions grow on mineral deficient soil." That statement seemed to be a fact. Commercial fertilizers had not been discovered. Even if the fertilizers had been available, we could not have afforded them.

Our summers were unbearably hot, dry and scoured by cyclones. The winters were long, hard, and for the most part, monotonous. The average snowfall was 30 inches, with blizzards and freezing temperatures.

When the territory was opened up for homesteaders in 1862, some 18,000 immigrants flooded the state each year to claim land. My parents went through many travails in order to raise twelve children in this very harsh land. We could all profit by paying attention to their great gifts of faith, love and sacrifice for their children.

It is to these parents of mine that this book is dedicated.

TABLE OF CONTENTS

"Brown bread is better, your body does not care
what color the bread is, only your mind does".
Ferne Chapman

INTRODUCTION — FOOLIN' WITH FOOD

Since early youth, food writing has been a part of my life. I developed a habit of making mental notes when cooking and writing out sketchy, random notes on any scrap of paper available. All of these ended in a scattered mass of observations and collected recipes. For the most part, my writing was done for relaxation, and as a diversion during the lean years. Later the habit turned into a compulsion to create new food dishes and new recipes.

My culinary expertise, as you might guess, began when I was trained to help to plant the garden, harvest the food and to cook for our family of fourteen. I practiced making meals for the country threshing crew, and for the community vagabonds and transients, who were plentiful during the Great Depression. The territory was inundated with people willing to work for food.

The teenagers of the 1940s were no less idealistic than the teenagers of the 1990s. I believed that I had already served my apprenticeship on the farm, butchering animals, and preparing meals for entire threshing crews. Therefore, I was not overjoyed to become a food clerk and a journeyman meat cutter in a Pacific Northwest supermarket at the age of 17; nor was I thrilled to become an apprentice cook in the U.S. Coast Guard Women's Reserve. As I look back, I have to admit that at least I had a well-paying job with good benefits, something today's teenagers would welcome.

It was long after our children were raised and had finished college that I had the special privilege to keep my 88-year-old invalid mother. She had numerous and severe infirmities at that time, and I took over her full-time care.

Even though I was employed full-time, my husband and I provided Lillian with super meals and a brighter outlook on life. Within seven months she had graduated from being housebound in a wheel chair to moving about with a walker. She became strong enough to walk to the living room for meals, and to enjoy an occasional outing.

Because my entire day off revolved around preparing food for Lillian, she approached me one day, peered over her glasses and spouted, ''My God, kid, every time I look at you, you are foolin' with food. Why don't you jot down a book and I will sign it.'' When I answered with, ''Mamma, you haven't been able to write for three years,'' (because of a tremor in her hands) she, without a moment's hesitation, snapped back, ''I'll practice.''

She wrote three pages filled to the edges with her full name—Lillian Blanche Carter. We picked the best of her writing and had her picture taken, ''just in case you want to use it,'' she said with a sly look on her face.

At the time it all sounded like so much "sky fodder" to me. My children, Jack and Lynne Chapman Gibbs, doggedly nudged me into enthusiastic pursuit of my joy in creating, baking and writing about wholesome food. After years of procrastinating, creating, and organizing, I finally set to work on a book.

In this book, I want to focus on nutrition. If good nutrition can reconstruct an 88-year-old body that appeared to be running in reverse, it can certainly help rebuild almost anyone.

When you think about cellular nutrition, think of it as a chain of life. Then think about the fact that a chain is only as strong as its weakest link. There are many nutrients needed in order to build good health besides proteins, carbohydrates, vitamins and minerals. Lipids and sterols are also ESSENTIAL to human health.

The "fat frenzy" may be encouraging too many people to ignore "essential" fatty acids. When choosing fats, it is good to try to balance the intake of saturated fats with unsaturated fats.

In selecting the recipes for this book, I wanted to present foods that are wholesome and provide the essential nutrients for a healthy body.

Enjoy.

Lillian Blanche Carter

Measuring

One of the first things to remember when baking is the proper measurement of ingredients. Our one hundred pound flour sack always arrived packed like a rock because it settled during transportation and handling. Never, to my knowledge, was the flour stirred before measuring. The oven or the yeast got the blame for "door-stop" loaves. Now we know that the flour must be shuffled, ruffled and stirred. For the best results use a dry-measure cup. Stir the flour and spoon it into the cup with a serving spoon. Arch the flour over the cup then, using the flat side of a spatula, slide the excess flour back into the container. The flat side of the spatula works best when measuring tiny yeast granules. The edge of the spatula will sometimes drag away too many granules.

Except where noted, all ingredients for the recipes in this book should be used at room temperature for best results.

BASIC MEASUREMENTS

1½ teaspoon = ½ Tablespoon	8 fluid ounces = 1 cup
3 teaspoons = 1 Tablespoon	16 fluid ounces = 2 cups
4 Tablespoons = ¼ cup	4 cups flour = 1 pound
5⅓ Tablespoons = ⅓ cup	2 cups granulated sugar = 1 pound
6 Tablespoons = ³/₈ cup, or	2¾ cups brown sugar = 1 pound
¼ cup + 2 Tablespoons	8 egg whites = 1 cup
8 Tablespoons = ½ cup	1 large egg = ¼ cup liquid
10 Tablespoons = ⁵/₈ cup, or	4 cups grated cheese = 1 pound
½ cup + 2 Tablespoons	1 cup nutmeats = 5 ounces
12 Tablespoons = ¾ cup	2 cups dates, cut = 1 pound
14 Tablespoons = ⁷/₈ cup	3 cups dried apricots = 1 pound
1 cup = 16 Tablespoons	1½ pound apples = 4 cups
1⅛ cup = 1 cup + 2 Tablespoons	1 cup uncooked rice or millet =
	2¼ cups cooked grain

Liquids

Using the best liquids available will be to no avail if the ingredients are improperly measured. Accurate liquid measurement becomes even more critical when using a bread machine. For tea breads, cakes, etc. even a few teaspoons of liquid could change the outcome of the recipe.

"Warm" water in this book should be between 105 and 115 degrees Fahrenheit. "Hot" water is 120 to 130 degrees.

It's no secret (to my friends at least) that potato water is the better water to use for bread making. It is not just boiled potato water. It is actually potato peeling water—the non-starch, mineral-laden portion of the potato. It is best to use organically grown potatoes.

Potato water

First scrub the organically grown potato and remove all blemishes. If the water is being used for white bread, use a potato peeler and scrape away some of the outside peeling. Then, using a paring knife, peel ¼-½-inch into the potato. Reserve the inside starch portion for thickening soups, stews and gravies. Cook and mash the peelings for the bread liquid. By using the potato and the liquid, the minerals, trace minerals and vitamin C are retained.

Fruit Juices

Fruit juices and purees from home-canned fruit can serve as both a portion of the sweetener and as a portion of the liquid. When purees are added, consider them as one third of the liquid called for in the recipe. When commercial fruit juices are added as liquid, dilute them with water if you're trying to avoid sugar. (Most commercial fruit juice contains corn syrup and other sweeteners.) Some fruit juices, such as apple and pineapple, can serve as part of the acid portion in the recipe. This is important when baking soda is called for in the recipe.

Milk Products

Milk products such as buttermilk, whole milk, nonfat milk, dry buttermilk, nonfat dry milk, powdered whey and powdered soy milk can all be used in these recipes. When substituting the dry products for fresh, add 1½-2 Tablespoons of the dry solids to 1 cup of water. If the recipe calls for milk and you substitute water, use only 7/8 cup. When replacing milk in a recipe, measure out 1 cup of the liquid to be used, remove 2 Tablespoons and add 2 Tablespoons polyunsaturated oil.

Nut-Seed Milk

Nut seed milk is an excellent addition to all baked goods. It can be considered a "superfood." It will add a portion of oil, solids, minerals, trace minerals and some vitamins to the recipe. All seeds and nuts can be used for making the milk. The heat from baking will destroy some of the vitamins, but the minerals and protein remain stable. Nuts like pecans, which are good sources of vitamin B-6, must be eaten fresh and raw for optimal benefits. Do not use roasted nuts to make nut milk.

¼ cup sunflower seeds, or sesame seeds 1 cup pineapple juice	¼ cup almonds 2 cups water

Soak the seeds and nuts for 3-4 hours, or overnight. Blend well in the blender. Add 1 more cup water, or pineapple juice. Add this additional liquid bit by bit, using the pulse setting on the blender. Strain. Use the liquid in the baked goods. Reserve the nuts and seeds. Use a small amount of them as a substitute with other chopped nuts in the recipe. The milk is a very perishable item. Freeze the remainder in ice cube trays. Place the cubes in a sealed bag and thaw them as needed.

   General Baking Information

Vegetable Mineral Water

Save all vegetable trimmings and refrigerate until a small bag is filled. Steam them in a small amount of water. Strain. Freeze the liquid in ice cube trays. Place the cubes in a sealed bag. Use one or two cubes in dark bread as a portion of the liquid. Do not use too many in one recipe, since the mineral water has a tart flavor.

Yeast And Leavening Agents

Bakers yeast is a live fungus which needs sugar in order to produce carbon dioxide. The more the dough is allowed to rise, the more carbon dioxide is trapped in the gluten. If you bake often, it is more economical to purchase yeast by the pound. Here in the Pacific Northwest we are able to purchase the Saf brand yeast at kitchen shops. Red Star active dry yeast is also sold by the pound, and both will work nicely in bread machines.

Baking soda is the least desirable leavening agents for these recipes. Baking soda destroys some of the B vitamins, in particular, Vitamin B-1 (thiamin). Thiamin is required by the body to metabolize carbohydrates. (Cereal grains used in breads are high-carbohydrate food items.) Instead of baking soda, try a double amount of low-sodium, double-acting baking powder. You can also make your own aluminum-free, salt-free leavening agent, using the recipe below.

1 part potassium bicarbonate (available at pharmacies, and somewhat more expensive)	2 parts cream of tartar 2 parts arrowroot powder

Blend with a whisk. Store in a sealed container.

Sweeteners

A very small amount of sweetener is needed to feed the yeast, and sugar contributes flavor and quality to baked goods. The choice of how much sugar or sweetener to add usually depends upon the type of bread being made. The sweet dough for cinnamon rolls, ceremonial breads and holiday breads calls for more sugar than sandwich loaves. The most commonly used sweeteners for bread making include:

honey	barley malt	maple syrup
diastatic malt	brown sugar	date sugar
white sugar	fruit puree and	fructose
rice bran syrup	fruit juice	

The ratio of sweetener for breadmaking is usually 1 teaspoon of sweetener per cup of flour. For muffins, 1 Tablespoon of sugar per cup of flour will make the kind of muffins that please the average palate. Artificial sweeteners are not acceptable and should be avoided.

Salt-Sodium

Sodium is a part of salt and found in most leavening agents. In bread, salt

(Continued next page)

helps control the yeast action and rising time, and condition the gluten. However, salt can usually be reduced in a recipe without impairing the end product. One-fourth teaspoon per cup of flour is adequate for most bread recipes. There are many different salt-sodium products on the market, all of which should be considered fair game. Some are better than others. Here are a few: Real salt comes from natural mineral rock salt deposits. Unrefined Atlantic Sea Salt is a slightly gray color. It contains many minerals and trace elements. Since it is pulverized, you can use less in recipes. Morton's Lite and Lowry's salt substitutes contain half the sodium found in table salt, with added potassium chloride. When the product is used in bread machine baking, the loaf results in a porous sponge-like texture. Therefore it would be better to use a smaller amount of one of the other salt substances.

When baking whole grain breads, you can substitute kelp, Irish moss or dulse in moderate amounts. They have the highest natural sodium content.

Fats, Essential Fatty Acids
Essential fatty acids are the beneficial components of fat that cannot be made by the body but are essential to human health. There are two categories: saturated and unsaturated fats. Unsaturated fats are liquid at room temperature. Polyunsaturated oils remain clear and fluid under refrigeration. Oils high in monounsaturated fats, such as peanut, soy and olive oil will become cloudy when refrigerated. The chemical make-up of the oils are designated by the different amounts of saturated, monounsaturated and polyunsaturated fat. Butter blended with a mixture of oils, lecithin, and sour cream appear to be more acceptable to the body's metabolism than hard, concentrated fat.
The Omega 6 oils are safflower oil, soy oil and corn oil. Omega 3 oil, which normally occurs in cold water fish, also appears in flax seed oil and in the flax seed. Walnut and soy oil contain small amounts of Omega 3.

To make oil blends, mix equal parts of peanut, safflower, and sunflower oil together in one large bottle and refrigerate.

Fat in recipes provide tenderness and volume to the product. Breads, with the exception of English muffins and French bread, should contain 1-2 teaspoons of oil per cup of flour. Muffins and quick breads need 1-2 Tablespoons of fat for good texture. For cakes, the minimum amount of fat for the best texture is 2 Tablespoons per cup of flour.

Soy Bean Lecithin
Lecithin is made from defatted soy beans. It is the best and most natural emulsifier used in the baking industry. Less oil can be used in the dough because the emulsifier splits the fat molecules and disperses them into the mass of dough. Oil and water do not mix—that is, until lecithin granules are added.

  General Baking Information

MIXES USED IN THIS BOOK

BASIC MUFFIN MIX

YIELD: 13 cups

6 cups unbleached
   white flour
6 cups whole wheat
   pastry flour
¼ cup oat bran or oat flour
¾ cup sugar

2 teaspoons vanilla powder
¼ cup whey powder, (optional)
3 Tablespoons sea salt
8 Tablespoons baking powder

Blend all of the ingredients. Stir well. Place in a sealed container.
Keep refrigerated or frozen. When ready to use, stir and measure the
needed amount and bring it to room temperature before mixing.

Note: 2 cups of mix, 1 cup liquid, 2-3 Tablespoons oil, and 1 egg will
result in a fine batch of muffins.

BASIC YEAST BREAD CONVENIENCE MIX

Note: This yeast Bread Convenience Mix is the most basic of the three
mixes. It will make a very nice loaf of bread, however, it contains only a
minimal amount of necessary nutrients.

YIELD: 15 cups, approx.

11 Tablespoons instant
    dry yeast
13 cups unbleached white flour
    or bread flour
⅔   cup sugar

1   cup nonfat dry milk
½   cup whey powder, (optional)
2   Tablespoons sea salt

Blend all the ingredients together. Cover and store in the refrigerator. Set
out the amount needed for your recipe 1 hour before using. Stir well
before measuring.

For bread add 1½ Tablespoons oil, 2½-3 cups all-purpose flour, 1 egg and
1¼ cups hot water.

DOUGH ENHANCER

Dough Enhancer is a commercial product designed to help dough rise. It is normally used in a 1-to-1 ratio to yeast in the recipe.

Here is a simple recipe for homemade dough enhancer:

¼ cup soy milk powder	2½ Tablespoons unbuffered vitamin C powder or crystals
¼ cup whey powder	
¼ cup dry vinegar	½ teaspoon ground ginger
¼ cup gluten	

Blend all ingredients. Seal in an airtight container. Use 1-2 Tablespoons for an average batch of bread.

PANCAKE AND WAFFLE MIX
WITH ROLLED OATS & CASHEWS

3 cups oatmeal, coarsely ground	5 cups all-purpose flour
2 cups buttermilk powder	½ cup sugar
2 teaspoons sea salt	3 Tablespoons baking powder
¼ cup soy flour	1 Tablespoon baking soda
¼ cup wheat germ	1½ cup cashews, coarsely ground
	¼ cup whole wheat flour

Using a whisk, blend the ingredients well. Seal and refrigerate.

WAFFLES: YIELD: 8-9 Waffles

3 eggs, seperated	2 cups milk, or buttermilk
¼ cup canola oil	2½ cups Pancake/Waffle Mix

Beat together the egg yolks, oil and liquid. In a seperate bowl beat the egg whites until stiff, but moist. Stir the flour into the liquid. Fold in the beaten egg whites. Bake.

PANCAKES:

1 egg	1 cup milk or fruit juice
2 Tablespoons canola oil	1½ cups Pancake/Waffle Mix

Beat the egg, oil and liquid together. Stir in the Pancake Mix. Bake on a hot oiled griddle until brown on both sides.

GRAIN-BIN GRANOLA

OVEN TIME: 1 hour at 250-300 Degrees   **YIELD:** 13-15 cups

2 cups oatmeal flakes, regular	AFTER COOKING:
2 cups spelt flakes	½ cup whey powder
2 cups rye flakes	⅓ cup nutritional yeast
1 cube butter, softened	⅔ cup wheat germ
¼ cup honey	½ cup flax seed, fresh,
¼ cup molasses	partially ground
⅓ cup Miller's bran	¼ cup lecithin granules

Blend the first seven ingredients. Heat and stir at intervals. When semi-crisp, add the second column of ingredients. Remove from the oven.

Prepare the following separately:
The nuts and dried fruit need not be heated; however, if they are, warm them separately. Nutrient losses are minimal when the food substance is heated whole, and at low temperatures.

¼ cup walnuts, chopped	¼ cup dates, snipped
¼ cup almonds	½ cup dried apricots, snipped
½ cup pecans, peanuts,	½ cup raisins
sunflower seeds,	or dried apples,
pumpkin seeds	peaches and pears
	can also be used

Blend all ingredients and refrigerate.

NOTE: It is best to separate the granola into smaller sealed containers and freeze, if it is not served often. The cereal makes a crunchy topping for ice cream and other desserts. Stir a Tablespoon or two into fruit-flavored yogurt for breakfast or lunch, or into cooked cereals such as oatmeal, spelt meal, farina, etc.

NEW GRAINS FORTIFIER MIX

½ cup amaranth
¼ cup EACH ground:
  flax seed, teff, pumpkin
  seeds, sunflower seeds and
  millet

PANTRY ENRICHMENT MIX

During the refining process, 20 or more nutrients are removed, or are reduced, depending upon the process used in the milling of the grain. Enriched breads have only four of the nutrients replaced. The bleaching process, coupled with the additives and preservatives, is not conducive to promoting good health.

When you spend precious time making bread, it should be created from the best possible ingredients. The bread must retain a good flavor, texture and an appetizing appearance.

The only thing that is better for dietary health than whole grain is a mixture of whole grain and nuts, seeds, and legumes. This inexpensive mix will enhance 12-15 batches of bread, depending upon the size of the batch of bread being made. For each 2 cups of flour called for in the recipe, add ¼-⅓ cup of the Enrichment Mix.

You can create a mix without using all the ingredients. The basic ratio of ingredients should be maintained, since some of the food items listed may add a pronounced flavor to the bread. It is best to start with fewer ingredients and experiment with more variety later.

If you wish all of the ingredients to be white, select the white and cream-colored food substances. Example: All of list number one, except, whole wheat flour. All of list number two, except flax, bran and rye flour. The choice for your pantry mix will depend upon the pocket book and individual taste.

FLOUR ADDITIONS:

1 CUP EACH:
- barley flour
- brown rice flour
- gluten
- nonfat dry milk
- oat flour
- oatmeal, regular
- quinoa
- soy flour
- spelt
- wheat germ
- whole wheat

¾ CUP EACH:
- amaranth
- corn, cracked, or cornmeal
- flax seed, whole
- kamut
- Miller's bran
- millet, cracked
- nutritional yeast
- rye
- whey powder
- yellow split peas, cracked

(Continued next page)

1/4 CUP EACH:
buckwheat (pungent and dark in color)
kelp powder (dark in color)
pumpkin seeds, cracked or ground
sesame seeds
sunflower seeds, cracked or ground
vitamin C crystals, unbuffered
wild rice (dark in color)

Blend all ingredients together. Seal in a gallon jar, or a large container
with a tight fitting lid. Refrigerate or freeze until ready to use. Use ¾ cup
to 1 cup mix for each 6-8 cups of flour called for in the recipe.

PIONEER-STYLE ENRICHMENT MIX

Note: This Pioneer Enrichment is best used when making whole grain dark
bread. By adding a variety of grains and other food substances, the bread
will be superior in quality. When the mix is added in small amounts, the
bread will be light-textured and flavorful. If a more robust loaf is desired,
add ⅓ cup of the Pioneer Mix for each two cups of flour called for in the
recipe.

1 cup measure of each:
   brown rice flour
   cornmeal
   Miller's bran
   oatmeal, regular
   rye flour
   spelt flour
   whole wheat flour

½ cup measure of each:
   nutritional yeast
   oat bran
   soy flour
   wheat germ
   whey powder

¼ cup measure each:
   vitamin C, unbuffered
   buckwheat flour or groats
   cocoa, optional
   gluten, optional
   pumpkin seeds, chopped
   wild rice, ground or cracked

Measure all ingredients into a very large bowl. Fold and stir well. Place in
a covered container. Refrigerate until ready to use. If you don't plan to use
the mix in a week or two, freeze it. The vitamin C and gluten build volume
in the bread dough.

ROBUST AND HEARTY MIX

2 cups oat flakes
2 cups wheat flakes
2 cups triticale flakes
2 cups kamut flakes
2 cups barley flakes
1 cup millet, coarsely ground

1 cup high-lysine cornmeal
2 teaspoons sesame seeds
¼ cup buckwheat groats
¼ cup sunflower
   seeds, cracked
¼ cup pumpkin
   seeds, cracked
2 Tablespoons kelp flakes

Mix all ingredients. Refrigerate or freeze until ready to use. Add 1 cup of the mixture for every 6-8 cups of flour used in the batch of bread.

RYE BREAD MIX

Note: This bread mix makes excellent loaves of bread. It can be used either in the bread machine or in an electric mixer. In order to eliminate too much bulk, some flour must be added when the bread is made. (See Rye and Cheese Rolls recipe.)

YIELD: 21 cups, approx.

12 Tablespoons instant
   dry yeast
9 cups bread flour
9 cups rye flour
2 cups whole wheat flour
¼ cup oat flour
1¼ Tablespoons vitamin C
   crystals, or powder
¼ cup flax seed

3 Tablespoons gluten
½ cup nonfat dry milk
⅓ cup soy flour
3 Tablespoons sea salt
4 Tablespoons caraway seed
3 Tablespoons anise seed
2 teaspoons ground ginger
½ cup oat flour
¾ cup sugar

Stir the flour and measure into a huge bowl. Add the remaining ingredients and blend well. Place the mixture in a sealed container and store in a cool place, or refrigerate. When ready to use, bring the needed amount to room temperature. Return the remainder to cold storage.

"Children can learn more by watching examples
than they can by preaching."
Edna Lister

SEVEN-GRAIN ENRICHMENT MIX

1 cup amaranth flour	3 Tablespoons flax seed
1 cup cornmeal	1 cup Miller's bran
2 cups oatmeal	1 cup oat bran
½ cup barley flour	

Other grain, nuts, or seeds may be added, if desired. Blend the ingredients together, seal and store in the refrigerator, or freezer. Remove the desired amount when ready to make bread. Use ¼-½ cup to each 6-8 cups flour used.

THREE-GRAIN YEAST BREAD MIX

Note: This mix will produce a spicy hot loaf. The ratio of spelt to wheat flour must be correct in order for the loaf to retain its rising power throughout the baking process. When complete spelt is used without gluten in the bread machine, the loaf will rise high, but it may shrink slightly toward the end of the baking process. This bread makes excellent sandwich bread, toast and croutons for a dinner salad garnish. In order to elimenate too much bulk, extra flour must be added when bread is mixed. See quick rolls recipe.

YIELD: 18 cups, approx.

7 cups bread flour	2 Tablespoons sea salt
5 cups whole wheat flour	15 Tablespoons instant
4 cups spelt flour	dry yeast
⅔ cup sugar	½ cup soy flour
¼ cup gluten	½ cup wheat germ

Stir and then measure all the flour before mixing in the remaining ingredients. Blend with a slotted spoon, or a whisk. Place them in a sealed container. Store in a cool place until needed. When ready to use remove the mixture from cold storage. Stir and measure the amount needed for the recipe. Let it come to room temperature before using. Add 2 cups mix plus 2¼ cups bread flour, 1¼ cups hot water, 1 egg and 1½ Tablespoons oil.

WHOLESOME MUFFIN MIX

YIELD: 13½-14 cups

6 cups unbleached white flour	½ cup sugar
6 cups whole wheat pastry flour	¼ cup soy milk powder, or
¼ cup barley flour	3 Tablespoons soy flour
¼ cup oat bran	¼ cup whey powder
1 cup nonfat dry milk	2 teaspoons vanilla powder
3 Tablespoons sea salt	8 Tablespoons baking powder

Blend all of the ingredients. Stir well. Place in a sealed container. Keep refrigerated or frozen. When ready to use, stir and measure out the needed amount. Bring it to room temperature before using.

Note: For simple muffins, use 2 cups Muffin Mix to 1 cup liquid, 1 egg, 1½ Tablespoons blended oil. (See Muffin section.)

YEAST BREAD CONVENIENCE MIX

Note: Every cook seems to be caught in a "time-deficiency syndrome." These quick mixes contain many more nutrients than can be found in any other packaged mix. This bread mix will cost less than a month's supply of cosmetics, and perhaps will create more beauty. For bread, add 1 cup of flour for each 1 cup of mix used.

YIELD: 18 cups, approx.

10 Tablespoons Saf yeast	2 teaspoons vitamin C crystals
11 cups bread flour	
1 cup nonfat dry milk	1-1¼ cups Millers bran
1 cup Pantry Enrichment mix	½ cup wheat germ
¼-½ cup gluten	½ cup whey powder
⅔ cup granulated sugar	2 Tablespoons sea salt
½ cup soy flour	½ cup barley or oat flour
⅓ cup nutritional yeast (see Quick Roll mix)	

Measure all ingredients into a very large bowl. Blend with electric beaters, a wire whip, or a long handled slotted spoon. Place in a covered container. Refrigerate or store in a very cool place. Freeze the mix if it is not utilized within a week or two.

YEAST BREADS

ANADAMA BREAD   Bread Of The Early American Settlers

NOTE: This is a modified version of an old settler's bread. Because millions of people eat delicate white bread, it is up to every caring nutritionist, cookbook writer and recipe gatherer to add back to the food as many nutrients as possible. The wide variety of ingredients used in this loaf do not substantially alter the color, flavor and texture of the bread. Both flavor and rising power remain good. The recipe can be adjusted for bread machine baking.

OVEN TIME: 30 minutes at 400 degrees   **YIELD:** 2 loaves

1	cup milk	2 Tablespoons soy milk powder
½	cup cornmeal	2 teaspoons sea salt
1	cup warm water	3 Tablespoons gluten
1	teaspoon sugar	2 Tablespoons whey powder
5	teaspoons instant dry yeast	2 Tablespoons wheat germ
2	Tablespoons dark molasses	2½ cups unbleached white flour
2	Tablespoons canola oil	3½-4 cups whole wheat flour

Heat the milk and sprinkle in the cornmeal. Remove from heat. Cool until warm to the touch.

In a large bowl or electric mixer bowl, dissolve the yeast in the warm water. Add the sugar. Stir to dissolve. Add 2 cups white flour. Beat 2 minutes. Scrape down the inside of the bowl.

Add the milk mixture, butter and molasses. Stir and beat.

In a separate bowl, blend together the remaining flour, soy milk powder, sea salt, gluten and whey powder. Gradually add the mixture to the batter. Scrape down the inside of the bowl.

When the dough leaves the side of the bowl, turn it out onto a sprinkling of flour. Knead 6-8 minutes or until the dough is smooth and elastic. Place the dough in an oiled bowl. Turn to coat all sides. Cover and let rise until doubled in bulk.

Press out the remaining air bubbles. Divide the dough into equal portions. Form the loaves. Place in sprayed or oiled loaf pans. Let rise until nearly doubled. Bake on the middle oven rack. Remove from the pan. Cool on a rack.

APPLE CIDER BREAD WITH OAT FLAKES

Note: This bread has a smooth pebbly appearance. It rises rapidly and has an excellent flavor and texture. Recently, oatmeal and oat bran have been touted as foods that help lower the high-density levels of cholesterol. This is a low-sugar, low-fat, low-salt bread.

OVEN TIME: 35 minutes at 375 degrees   **YIELD:** 2 loaves

1 cup apple cider, warm	1 Tablespoon instant dry yeast
½ cup oat flakes	1 Tablespoon sugar
2 Tablespoons canola oil	¾ cup zucchini-apple puree
2½ teaspoons sea salt	2 cups unbleached white flour
1 cup warm water	5-5½ cups whole wheat flour
or potato water	

In a small saucepan, bring the apple cider to a simmer. Stir in the oat flakes. Remove from the heat and set aside. Stir in the salt and the oil. Cool until warm to the touch.

In large bowl or electric mixer bowl, dissolve yeast and add in the warm cider mixture. Add the sugar and let the mixture rest until foamy. With the dough hook in place, beat in 2 cups white flour. Beat 2 minutes. Add the apple cider/oatmeal mixture and the apple zucchini puree. Mix well. Gradually add the remaining flour, beating after each addition. Scrape the sides of the bowl at intervals. When the dough begins to pull away from the sides of the bowl, turn it out onto a sprinkling of flour. Knead the dough for 6-8 minutes, until smooth and elastic. Place it in an oiled bowl. Turn the oil side up. Cover with wax paper and a cloth. Let rise until doubled in bulk.
Press out the air bubbles and divide in half. Form the loaves and place in well-greased or sprayed pans. Let rise a bit over the pan. Bake. Cool on a rack.

Tip: Bread to heavy? It may be due to; the wrong type of flour, old flour, too short a rising time, underkneading or too cool during the rising time

BASIC BROWN BREAD

Note: This recipe makes an excellent practice dough for the novice bread maker. It is nearly impossible to ruin this batch of bread. Lukewarm water, beating and kneading are the three keys to making this outstanding batch of bread.

OVEN TIME: 25-30 minutes at 375 degrees   **YIELD:** 2 large loaves

1½ cups milk, scalded	1½ cups potato water, or warm water
½ cup brown sugar	2 Tablespoons instant dry yeast
¼ cup + 1 Tablespoon safflower oil	1 Tablespoon sugar
2 Tablespoons sea salt	7-8 cups whole wheat flour
⅓ cup dark molasses	1½-2 cups all-purpose flour

In a small saucepan scald the milk and add the next 4 ingredients. Remove from the heat and cool until warm to the touch. In a large bowl or an electric mixer bowl, dissolve the yeast in the warm water or potato water and add the sugar. Let rest until foamy. Beat in 2 cups of whole wheat flour, beating for 5 minutes. Let the "sponge" rest until bubbly. Add the milk mixture and stir together. Add the remaining flour in small amounts, beating after each addition. Scrape down the sides of the bowl. When the dough clings to the side of the bowl, turn the dough out on a flat surface onto a sprinkling of flour. Knead well. Place the dough in an oiled bowl. Turn the oil side up. Cover and let rise until doubled in bulk.

Knead the dough down. Turn out on a flat surface and press out the remaining air bubbles. Divide the dough and let rest for 6-8 minutes. Form the loaves. Place in greased pans. Cover and let rise until nearly doubled in bulk. If desired, brush the top of the loaves with oil, for a soft crust, or with egg white and water for a shiny crust. Bake.

Note: Since the bread will rise a bit more in the oven, do not allow it to rise too high over the edge of the pan before placing it in the oven. If gluten flour is used in this recipe, reduce oven temperature by 10 degrees. The gluten browns faster and darker. This dough is perfect for dinner rolls.

Dry crumbly bread can be the result of to much flour, oven heat to low or insufficient kneading.

BEETS 'N RYE BREAD

"Can you beet that!"
(A Chase Lake Community Favorite)

Note: This bread was exciting for us for two reasons. First, food and cash were both scarce on the farm, which meant every edible food was fair game for bread. Second, the color, flavor and texture of this bread can't be beat. The beet relish gives this loaf a sweet and sour flavor; however, before adding the relish to the bread, it must be heated to simmering. If this is not done, the live enzymes in the beets will digest the gluten, making the batter runny. Beet pickles may be used without this danger, since they have already been heated. The vinegar in the beets enhances the rising power of the dough.

Oven Time: 35-40 minutes at 375 degrees   **YIELD:** 2 loaves

1 cup potato water	2 teaspoons dry instant yeast
¼ cup rye flakes	2 Tablespoons brown sugar
2 teaspoons caraway seed	2 Tablespoons molasses
½ teaspoon anise seed	1 Tablespoon orange zest
3 Tablespoons butter	1½ teaspoons sea salt
½ cup beet pickles, or beet relish	4 cups Three Grain bread mix
1 cup buttermilk	2 cups rye flour
¼ cup warm water	1 Tablespoon fennel seeds

In a small saucepan heat the potato water. Stir in the rye flakes, caraway seeds, anise seeds, butter, beet pickle puree and buttermilk. Remove from the heat. Cool until warm to the touch. Set aside. Dissolve the yeast in the ¼ cup warm water. Add it to a large bowl or an electric mixer bowl, then add the brown sugar. If time allows, let the mixture rest until bubbly. Add the cooked mixture. Stir in 2 cups bread mix. Beat for 2 minutes. Add the molasses, orange zest and sea salt. Beat well. In another small bowl blend together the rye flour and the remaining bread mix.

Scrape down the inside of the bowl. When dough begins to pull away from the sides of the bowl, turn it out onto a sprinkling of flour. Knead until the dough becomes smooth and elastic. Shape it into a ball. Place in an oiled bowl. Turn to coat all sides with oil and cover with wax paper and a cloth. Let rise until doubled in bulk. Punch down. (If time allows, let rise again.)

Yeast Bread

Turn the dough out onto a sprinkling of flour. Press out the remaining air bubbles. Divide the dough. Let rest for 10 minutes. Form the loaves. Place in an oiled pan on a sprinkling of cornmeal. Let rise until nearly doubled in bulk. Brush with the egg white and water mixture. Sprinkle with cracked rye berries or sunflower seeds. Bake.

COUNTRY RAW BEET RELISH

3 raw beets, scrubbed, grated
1 medium onion, grated
¼ cup raw honey
   horseradish

¼ cup sunflower seed oil
⅓ cup apple cider vinegar
1 Tablespoon prepared
½-1 teaspoon sea salt
   Pepper to taste

Prepare and blend all ingredients. Place in a tightly covered container. Stir occasionally. Keep refrigerated. Steam for 4-5 minutes before adding the relish to the bread.

"Soul is that part of the spirit which
has all the qualities of God!"
Edna Lister

"Endeavor is better than a Million Promises"
Ferne Chapman

BOHEMIAN RYE BREAD

Note: Chase Lake community farmers, seemingly forgotten by the outside world, depended upon one another for both physical and emotional support. When our winter stores of grain were low the neighboring farmers and the local merchants always came to the rescue. Many times we would have only one cereal grain left among us all in the granary. It seemed that rye was the last to be used.

Oven Time: 35-40 minutes at 375 degrees   **YIELD:** 2 loaves

1 cup potato water	½ teaspoon cardamom
1 Tablespoon instant dry yeast	2 teaspoons caraway seed
3 Tablespoons brown sugar	½ teaspoon ginger
¼ cup molasses	1 cup chopped onion
¾ cup sour cream	½ cup oat flour or oat bran
3 Tablespoons butter	2 cups whole wheat flour
2 teaspoons sea salt	1½-2 cups rye flour

In a small frying pan, saute the onion in 1 Tablespoon olive oil. Set aside. Heat the potato water, then pour it into a large bowl or an electric mixer bowl. Add the yeast and dissolve. Add the brown sugar. If time allows, let rest until bubbly. Add the molasses and sour cream. Beat in the wheat flour. Beat 2 minutes. Scrape down the inside of the bowl. Add the sauteed onion. In a small bowl, blend the oat flour, rye flour with the herbs and sea salt. Gradually add it to the batter. Beat after each addition.

When the dough begins to leave the side of the bowl, turn it out in a sprinkling of flour. Knead until the dough becomes smooth and elastic. Shape the dough into a ball. Place it in an oiled bowl. Turn to oil all sides. Cover with wax paper and a cloth. Let rise in a warm place until doubled in bulk.

Press out air bubbles. Divide the dough. Let rest for 10 minutes. Form round loaves. Place in oiled round pans. Let rise until nearly doubled in bulk. Cut shallow slits in the top with a sharp knife. Brush with a mixture of egg white and water. Sprinkle the loaves with corn meal, or sunflower seeds. Bake at 400 degrees for 10 minutes. Reduce the heat to 375 degrees and finish the baking cycle. When the loaves are finished, remove it from the pans. Cool on a rack.

Note: Putting cheese sticks in the center of the loaf adds color and nutrition. You can also replace the sour cream with plain yogurt.

 Yeast Bread

BRANDON'S BURGER BUNS

Note: The national palate of Americans, young and old alike, has set every mother scampering to squeeze more nutrients into the sandwich. Since Brandon Lee does not like cheese on his "burger," we hide cottage cheese in the hamburger buns. So far his keen sense of smell has not shot down our plan.

OVEN TIME: 30 minutes at 400 degrees   **YIELD:** 12-14 buns

1 cup water	1 cup warm milk
1 small potato	1 Tablespoon lemon juice
5 teaspoons instant dry yeast	1 egg
2 Tablespoons sugar	1 teaspoon sea salt
½ cup cottage cheese	1 Tablespoon gluten
2 Tablespoons blended oil	¼ cup Enrichment Mix
	8½-9 cups unbleached white flour, or all-purpose flour

Cook the potato in 1 cup of water. Mash it in the cooking water. Remove from the heat. Cool to warm.

Turn it into a large bowl, or an electric mixer bowl. Add the yeast and dissolve. Add the sugar. Beat in 2 cups of flour. Beat 2 minutes. In the blender, puree the cottage cheese in the milk and lemon juice. Add it to the yeast mixture. Beat in the egg. Scrape down the bowl. Stir the gluten and the Enrichment Mix into the remaining flour. Gradually add the mixture to the batter. Scrape down the inside of the bowl. When the dough leaves the side of the bowl, turn it out onto a sprinkling of flour. Knead 6-8 minutes, or until the dough is smooth and elastic.

Place the dough in an oiled bowl. Turn to coat all sides. Cover and let rise until doubled in bulk.

Press out the remaining air bubbles. Pat or roll the dough into a rectangle, ¾-1 inch thick. Cut with a 3-inch cookie cutter. Place the buns on a prepared baking pan. Gather together the small pieces of dough. Roll out and cut the remainder into buns. Cover. Let rise until nearly doubled in bulk. Brush with a mixture of egg white whisked in water. Sprinkle with sesame seeds, or poppy seeds, if desired.

Bake. When the buns are finished, remove them from the pan. Cool on a rack.

BREANNA'S TEDDY BEAR BREAD

Note: This pliable smooth dough was the same type we used as children to create animal art. We gathered around the old oak table while Mamma kneaded the "big batch" of bread. It was all part of our creative home entertainment, particularly during the winter months.

OVEN TIME: 30-35 minutes at 375 degrees   **YIELD:** 2 bears

½ cup milk, scalded	¼ cup non-fat dry milk
¼ cup butter	5½-6 cups bread flour
1½ cups warm water, or potato water	1 cup whole wheat flour
2 Tablespoons instant dry yeast	¼ cup wheat germ
2 teaspoons salt	1 egg, beaten
2 eggs	1-2 Tablespoons milk
	6 Tablespoons Miller's Bran Raisins for the eyes and buttons

In a small saucepan, scald the milk. Remove from the heat, stir in the butter and cool until warm to the touch. In a large bowl or electric mixer bowl, dissolve the yeast in the warm water or potato water. Add the sugar. Let rest until foamy. Beat in 2 cups flour. Beat for 2 minutes. Let the "sponge" rest until bubbly. Beat in the eggs, one at a time. Add the milk mixture and salt. Stir and blend.

In a separate bowl, blend the dry milk, wheat germ and whole wheat flour. Add to the sponge. Gradually add the remaining flour. Beat after each addition. Scrape down the inside of the bowl.

When the dough leaves the side of the bowl; turn the dough out on a flat surface onto a sprinkling of flour. Knead until smooth and elastic. Place the dough in an oiled bowl. Turn to coat all sides. Cover and let rise until doubled in bulk. Knead the dough down. Turn out on a flat surface and press out the remaining air bubbles. Divide the dough into 4 equal portions. Roll 2-4 inch balls for the bodies. Cut one portion in half. Roll for the heads. Cut one into 14 pieces for the arms, legs, noses and ears. Round each piece in your palms. Assemble the bear on an oiled baking sheet. Brush each piece with the milk-egg mixture. Dab each piece into the Miller's bran, then pinch it to the body in its proper place. (Brush with more of the egg mixture if needed.) Arrange the eyes, and buttons. Cover and let rise until nearly doubled in bulk. Press an indentation in the ears and insert a raisin or a chocolate chip. Dab with the egg mixture before placing the bears in the oven. Bake. Let the bear cool slightly before removing to a rack.

  Yeast Bread

BROWN BETTY BATTER BREAD

Note: All Americans love the old-fashioned Apple Brown Betty Dessert. This quick batter bread can satisfy your sweet tooth, and it has only one-fourth the sugar and fat content of traditional apple brown betty dessert.

OVEN TIME: 30 minutes at 375 degrees   **YIELD:** 2 loaves

1½ cup milk, scalded	½ cup warm water
3 Tablespoons oatmeal	1 teaspoon sugar
2 Tablespoons butter	2 eggs
¾ cup apples, diced	5½-6 cups unbleached white flour
¼ cup brown sugar	2 Tablespoons butter
1 teaspoon sea salt	¼ cup brown sugar
1 teaspoon cinnamon	3 Tablespoons oatmeal
2 Tablespoons instant dry yeast	¼ cup pecans, chopped

In a small saucepan, heat the milk. Add the oatmeal, butter, apples, brown sugar, sea salt and cinnamon. Remove from the heat. Set aside. Cool until warm to the touch.

In a large bowl or electric mixer bowl, dissolve the yeast in the warm water and add 1 teaspoon sugar. Add the warm milk mixture. Blend. Scrape down the inside of the bowl. Add 3½ cups flour. Beat 2 minutes. Add the eggs, one at a time, beat after each addition. Scrape down the inside of the bowl. Cover and let rise for 30 minutes in the mixing bowl. Stir down.

Beat in the remaining flour. When the dough becomes stiff and tacky, cover and let rise again until doubled in bulk.

Stir down and spoon into 2 oiled loaf pans. Push the batter well into the corners of the pans. Poke small holes in the top of the batter with a sharp knife. Insert small pieces of chopped apple and nuts. In a small bowl, mix the topping mixture.

Sprinkle the topping mixture over the loaves. Let rise until nearly doubled in bulk. Place on the middle rack of the oven. Bake. When the bread is finished, remove it from the pan. Cool on a rack.

BUCKWHEAT POTATO BREAD

Note: This chestnut-colored loaf has a crisp crust, a fine smooth texture and a nutty flavor. It is an exceptional addition to a buffet luncheon, particularly when served with tangy smoked meat slices, such as corned beef, ham and salami.

OVEN TIME: 30-35 minutes at 375 degrees　　**YIELD:** 2 loaves

1 cup water	2 teaspoons lecithin granules
1 small potato, cubed	½ cup warm water
2 Tablespoons whole buckwheat	2 Tablespoons instant dry yeast
2 teaspoons sea salt	2 Tablespoons brown sugar
1 cup milk, scalded	2 eggs
3 Tablespoons dark molasses	2½ cups bread flour, or all-purpose flour
3 Tablespoons sunflower seed oil	1¼ cups buckwheat flour
½ teaspoon ginger	2-2½ cups whole wheat flour

In a small sauce pan cook the first 3 ingredients together. Mash. Stir in the next 6 ingredients. Cool until warm to the touch.

In a large mixing bowl or an electric mixer bowl, dissolve the yeast in the warm water. Add the brown sugar. Add the potato mixture. Add 2 cups bread flour. Beat 2 minutes. Add the buckwheat flour. Beat. Scrape down the sides of the bowl. Gradually add the remaining flour, beating after each addition.

When the dough begins to leave the inside of the bowl. Turn out onto a sprinkling of flour. Knead 5-6 minutes, until the dough is smooth and elastic. Place in an oiled bowl. Turn to oil all sides of dough. Cover and let rise until doubled in bulk.

Press air bubbles from dough. Divide and form the loaves. Place in well greased loaf pans. Let rise until slightly above the top of the pan. Brush the tops with a mixture of 1 egg white and 1 Tablespoon of water. Designs may be carefully cut diagonally on each loaf. Bake. Cool on racks.

"All conflict comes from the subconscious belief
in two powers, God and self."
Edna Lister

CHEDDAR, BEAN AND BACON BREAD

Note: This bread can be finished quickly after the beans are sprouted (if sprouting is desired). The sprouting process will make the beans cook rapidly and will partially predigest the phytates in the legumes. Cheese, beans, and bacon have long been one of America's favorite meal-mates. Expect a perfect flavor, good texture and increased nutritional value in this bread.

OVEN TIME: 35 minutes at 400 degrees　　**YIELD:** 3 loaves

2 cups warm water	2 Tablespoons soybean oil
2 Tablespoons instant dry yeast	¼ cup wheat germ
6-7 strips lean bacon	¼ cup Miller's bran
1 cup bean broth	¾ cup baked bean puree
¼ cup sugar	7-8 cups bread flour or unbleached white flour
1 Tablespoon sea salt	1½ cups Sharp Cheddar cheese, grated
½ teaspoon vitamin C	

Prepare the bacon. Drain on dry bread crusts or on paper towels. Set aside. Puree the baked beans. Set aside.

In a mixing bowl or an electric mixer bowl, dissolve the yeast in the warm water. Add 2 teaspoons of the sugar. Let the mixture rest until foamy. Stir in the bean liquid. Add 3 cups flour. Beat 2 minutes. Add the remaining sugar, sea salt, vitamin C, soy oil and crumbled bacon. Stir to blend. Add the bean puree and the grated cheese. Scrape the inside of the bowl.

In a separate bowl, blend the remaining flour, wheat germ and bran. Gradually add this mixture to the batter. When the dough begins to leave the sides of the bowl, turn the dough out in a sprinkling of flour.

Knead for 6-8 minutes or until the dough is elastic and pliable. Place it in an oiled bowl, turn to coat all sides of the dough with oil. Cover and let rise until doubled in bulk.

Turn the dough out on an oiled surface. Press out the remaining air bubbles. Divide the dough and form the loaves. Place in oiled or sprayed loaf pans. Let rise until doubled in bulk. Brush tops lightly with egg mixture. Bake. Remove from the pans. Cool on racks.

CHORIZO WHOLE GRAIN BREAD

Note: Breadmaking has changed considerably in the past decade. There are more grains available than ever before. Breadmaking becomes even more exciting when the grain is ground just prior to baking. The warm flour from the grinder, coupled with electric mixer beating, can cut the preparation time in half.

OVEN TIME: 35 minutes at 375 Degrees   **YIELD:** 2 large loaves

1 pound chorizo	3 Tablespoons gluten
1 medium onion, minced	1 teaspoon sea salt
5 teaspoons instant yeast	1 cup Sharp Cheddar cheese, grated
1 cup warm water	2/3 cup Parmesan, cheese, grated
3 Tablespoons honey	7 cups whole wheat flour
2½ cups warm milk	

In a medium-sized skillet, crumble the chorizo into the pan. Saute. Remove from the pan and drain on paper towels or dry bread crusts. Wipe the pan free of the chorizo oil. Saute the onion in 1 Tablespoon olive oil. Remove the onion from the pan, set aside to drain. Heat the milk in a medium saucepan. Remove from the heat. Cool until warm to the touch.

In a large bowl or electric mixer bowl, dissolve the yeast in the water and add the milk and honey. Add 4 cups white flour. Beat 2 minutes. Scrape down the inside of the bowl. Add the chorizo and onion. Blend well. Add the Parmesan cheese and ¼ cup of the Cheddar cheese. Blend. Scrape down the inside of the bowl. Blend the gluten and sea salt with the whole wheat flour. Gradually add it to the batter. When the dough leaves the side of the bowl, turn it out in a sprinkling of flour. Knead until the dough is smooth and elastic. Place it in an oiled bowl. Turn the dough to coat all sides. Cover and let rise until doubled in bulk.

Punch down. Turn out on a flat surface. Press out the remaining air bubbles. Knead in the remaining cheese. Divide the dough into equal portions. Form the loaves. Place in oiled baking pans. Let rise to nearly doubled in bulk. Bake. When the bread is finished, remove it from the pans. Cool on a rack.

"As you believe, it shall be done unto you."
Matthew 8:13

CORNMEAL AND YELLOW SPLIT PEA BREAD

Note: This mixture of corn and yellow split peas is a colorful sun-shiny loaf. The rising power is excellent and the combination of the mingled flavors makes a great sandwich for brown baggers.

OVEN TIME: 30 minutes at 400 degrees   **YIELD:** 3 large loaves

1	cup whole milk	3	Tablespoons sugar or honey
⅔	cup evaporated milk	2½	teaspoons sea salt
3	cups warm water	3	Tablespoons safflower oil
¼	cup yellow split pea meal	8-9	cups all-purpose flour
¼	cup cornmeal	1	egg white, beaten
5	teaspoons instant dry yeast	2	Tablespoons water

In small saucepan heat the milk with the evaporated milk and 1 cup of the water. Stir in the split pea meal and cornmeal. Remove from heat when the mixture begins to boil. Cool until warm to the touch. In a large bowl or electric mixer bowl, dissolve yeast in remaining warm water.
Add the sugar. Add 2 cups flour. Beat 2 minutes.

Add the oil, salt and cornmeal mixture. Stir and blend. Add 3 cups of flour. Beat 2 minutes. Gradually add the remaining flour. When the dough begins to leave the sides of the bowl, turn it out in a sprinkling of flour. Knead until the dough becomes smooth and elastic. Sprinkle a bit more flour over the dough if needed. Shape into ball and place it in an oiled bowl. Turn to coat all sides of the dough. Cover and let rise in warm place until doubled in bulk.

Punch down. Divide the dough in half. Form into loaves. Place in oiled pans which have been sprinkled with cornmeal. Let rise until nearly doubled in bulk. Brush the top of the loaves with the egg white mixture. Sprinkle with cornmeal. Loaves may be baked in a round pan, if desired. Bake the loaves on the middle rack of the oven. When the loaves are finished, remove from the pans. Cool on a rack. Serve with garlic or lecithin butter.

LECITHIN BUTTER:
1 pound butter, unsalted, 3 Tablespoons non-fat dry milk, 4 Tablespoons lecithin granules, 3 Tablespoons safflower oil.

Blend the room temperature ingredients together. Rrefrigerate in sealed containers.

COTTAGE CHEESE DILL BREAD

Note: The cottage cheese and onion particles not only lend character to the appearance of this bread, but these flavors are heightened because of the dill weed. Soy flour adds extra protein and allows the bread to brown quickly.

OVEN TIME: 35-40 minutes at 375 degrees   **YIELD:** 3 round loaves

1 cup cottage cheese	1 Tablespoon soy flour
3 Tablespoons whey powder	2 Tablespoons gluten flour
2 cup warm water	2 Tablespoons millet flour
2 Tablespoons instant dry yeast	4 teaspoons sea salt
¼ cup sugar	⅔ cup onion, raw diced
7½-8 cups unbleached white flour	2 teaspoons dill weed
1 egg	¼ cup sunflower seed oil

In a medium bowl combine 1 cup of the unbleached flour with the soy, gluten, and millet flours. Set aside. Place 1 cup water in the blender and add the cottage cheese and whey powder. Puree. Set aside.
In large bowl or electric mixer bowl, dissolve yeast in the remaining cup of warm water. Add 2 teaspoons of the sugar. Stir until dissolved. Add the cottage cheese puree. Add three cups of flour. Beat 2 minutes. Add the remaining sugar, egg, sea salt, onion, dill weed and oil. Stir in the blended flours. Add the remaining flour in small amounts, until the dough is elastic and easy to handle.
Make a large ball of the dough. Place it into an oiled bowl. Turn to coat all sides with oil. Cover with wax paper and a cloth. Let rise until doubled in bulk.
Punch down. Turn out on an oiled surface. Knead 6-8 minutes. Divide dough into equal portions. Form each into a round loaf. Place the loaves in oiled round baking pans. Cover. Let rise until nearly doubled in bulk. Bake. Remove from the pans. Cool on a rack. Serve with Garlic Dilly Butter.

GARLIC DILLY BUTTER:
1 cube soft butter, ¼ teaspoon dill weed, 2 Tablespoons sunflower oil, 1 teaspoon garlic powder, and 2 teaspoons non-fat dry milk.

Combine all ingredients and beat with an electric mixer.
Serve on warm bread.

   Yeast Bread

COUNTRY CRACKLIN' BREAD

Note: In rural America during the Great Depression, almost everything that we ate was prepared in our own kitchen. The pork "cracklins" in this bread recipe were cooked in the wood stove oven on butchering day. The pork skin, with the fat intact, was cubed and placed in a large pan. It was baked until all the fat was rendered. It was then strained through bleached flour sack material. The fat was removed from the heavy skin and ground, or diced.

OVEN TIME: 30 minutes at 375 Degrees   **YIELD:** 1 loaf

1 cup potato water	2 teaspoons mineral salt
¼ cup oatmeal	1 cup fresh ground cracklins
1 cup warm skim milk	3 Tablespoons cornmeal
1 Tablespoons instant dry yeast	3½ cups all-purpose flour
2 Tablespoons sugar	2½-3 cups whole wheat flour
1 egg	2 Tablespoons cornmeal

In a small sauce pan, cook 1 small potato in the water. Mash in the cooking water, stir in the oatmeal and milk. Set aside. Cool until warm to the touch. Add the warm mixture to a large bowl or electric mixer bowl, add the yeast and sugar, stir to dissolve. Let rest until foamy, if time allows.

Beat in 3 cups of white flour.
Beat in the egg and cracklins. In a separate small bowl, blend together 3 Tablespoons cornmeal, salt and remaining flour. Gradually add the remaining dry ingredients. Beat after each addition. Scrape down the inside of the bowl. When the dough begins to clean the side of the bowl, turn it out in a sprinkling of flour. Knead until smooth and elastic. Place the dough in an oiled bowl. Turn to coat all sides of the dough with oil. Cover and let rise until doubled in bulk.

Knead down. Turn out on a flat surface, press out the remaining air bubbles. Let rest for 2-3 minutes. Spray or oil the loaf pan and dust with cornmeal. Form into a loaf or into dinner rolls. Place in an oiled loaf pan. Cover with a light cloth. Let rise to slightly over the top of the pan. Bake. When the loaf is finished, brush the top with oil, or sweet cream.

"Somewhere on the back burner of our soul, there is something going on; let's find out what that is."
David Mahalic

Yeast Bread   29

DARCEA'S SPELT AND OAT BREAD

Note: This bread is created from two of the alternative grains which may help those individuals who are sensitive to wheat. Even though spelt is a second cousin to wheat, its different chromosome patterns seem to agree with most of the allergy-prone population.

OVEN TIME: 30-35 minutes at 400 degrees   **YIELD:** 2 loaves

1 cup water	500 milligrams vitamin C
½ cup raw potato	3 Tablespoons molasses
⅓ cup spelt flakes	2 teaspoons sea salt
3 Tablespoons butter	2 Tablespoons barley flour
2 cups warm water	3 Tablespoons soy flour
2 Tablespoons instant dry yeast	1 cup oat flour
3 Tablespoons honey	6-7 cups spelt flour

Peel the scrubbed potato and dice. Measure ½ cup. Cook in 1 cup of water. Mash. Add spelt flakes and butter to the hot liquid. Cool until warm to touch.

In a large bowl or electric mixer bowl, dissolve the yeast in the warm water. Add the honey and molasses. Add 3 cups of spelt flour. Beat 2 minutes. Scrape down the inside of the bowl. Stir in the vitamin C.

In a separate bowl, blend the sea salt, soy flour, barley flour, oat flour, and the remaining spelt flour. Gradually add the mixture to the batter. Beat after each addition. Scrape down the inside of the bowl. When the dough begins to climb the dough hook, turn it out on a flat surface onto a sprinkling of flour. Knead well.

Place the dough in an oiled bowl. Turn the dough to oil all sides. Cover. Let rise until doubled in bulk. Punch down the dough. Turn out on a flat surface. Press out the remaining air bubbles. Divide the dough. Let it rest for 6-8 minutes. Form the loaves and place in oiled pans. Cover and let rise until nearly doubled in bulk. If desired, brush the top of the loaves with oil for soft crust, or with 1 egg white whisked in 1 Tablespoon water. Bake. When the loaves are finished, remove from the pan. Cool on a rack.

Note: The oat flour, soy flour and barley flour can be replaced with 1¼ cups plus 1 Tablespoon of the Pantry Enrichment mix.

DATE OAT YEAST BREAD

Note: Recent research suggests that oat bran may assist in lowering high-density cholesterol. This alone can make oat bran fair game for bread, pastries and cereal. The star qualities of oat products are their minerals, trace minerals and protein, all of which are required for good health.

OVEN TIME: 30 minutes at 400 degrees   **YIELD:** 3 loaves

½ cup dates, minced	¼ cup oat bran
1 cup sour milk	½ cup old fashioned oatmeal
4 teapoons Saf yeast	1 egg
3 cups warm water	4-4½ cups unbleached white flour
3 Tablespoons honey	3 cups whole wheat flour
2 Tablespoons sea salt	1 Tablespoon Dough
¼ cup sunflower seed oil	Enhancer, (optional)
1 Tablespoon lemon juice	

Soak dates in sour milk. Set aside.

In a large mixing bowl or electric mixer bowl, dissolve the yeast the in warm water and add the honey. Add 3 cups white flour. Beat 2 minutes. Add the date mixture. Stir in the sea salt, sunflower seed oil and lemon juice. Scrape down the inside of the bowl.

In a separate bowl, blend together the oat bran, oatmeal, Dough Enhancer and the remaining flour. Reserve. Add the egg. Beat. Gradually stir in the remaining dry ingredients. When the dough leaves the sides of the bowl, turn the dough out onto a sprinkling of flour. Knead until the dough is smooth and elastic. If dough becomes too sticky to handle, add a few sprinkles of flour.

Place dough in an oiled bowl. Turn the dough to coat all sides with oil. Cover with wax paper and a cloth. Let rise until doubled in bulk. Turn out on an oiled surface and press out the remaining air bubbles. Divide dough into equal portions. Let it rest 8-10 minutes. Form into loaves. Place in oiled loaf pans. Let rise until nearly doubled. Bake. When the loaves are finished remove from the pans. Cool on a rack. Brush tops with oil or sweet cream.

"Learn to become that which you demand others to be."
Edna Lister

DIET BREAD

Note: When it comes to dieting, everyone looks for the food substances which benefit weight loss programs, namely those foods that are lower in calories and still furnish both energy and fiber. Dried fruit and vegetable pulp are excellent for adding fiber to homemade bread.

OVEN TIME: 35-40 minutes at 375 degrees   **YIELD:** 1 loaf

1½ cups warm potato water, or skim milk	1 Tablespoon cider vinegar
2 teaspoons Saf yeast	1 teaspoon sea kelp
1 teaspoon honey	¼ cup Miller's bran or oat bran
1 Tablespoon sour cream	1 cup dried carrot pulp
¼ teaspoon unbuffered vitamin C	3 cups gluten flour
	¼ cup buckwheat flour
	½ cup whole wheat flour

In a large bowl or electric mixer bowl, dissolve the yeast in the warm potato water or warm skim milk. Add the honey. If time allows, let the mixture rest until foamy. Add 2 cups gluten flour. Beat 2 minutes. Stir the sour cream, vinegar and vitamin C together and add to the batter. Blend. Scrape down the inside of the bowl.

In a separate bowl, blend the remaining flour with the Miller's bran and sea kelp. Gradually add it to the batter. Beat. When the dough leaves the side of the bowl, turn it out onto a sprinkling of flour. Knead until smooth and elastic. Make a ball of the dough and place it in an oiled bowl. Turn to coat all sides. Cover and let rise until doubled in bulk.

Punch down. If time allows, let the bread rise once more. Turn the dough out and press out the remaining air bubbles. Form the loaf and place in an oiled baking pan. Let rise until nearly doubled in bulk. The loaf will look elegant if you slash a design in the top with a knife. Brush with egg white whisked in water. Sprinkle with quick oats, sesame seeds, or caraway seeds. Bake. When the loaf is baked, remove it from the pan. Cool on a rack. Serve thinly sliced.

"Resolve to keep happy and your joy shall form a shield against difficulty"
Edna Lister

 Yeast Bread

DOUBLE CRUNCH MILLET BREAD

Note: The marriage of these fine cereal grains makes an excellent sandwich bread. The cooked millet creates creamy-yellow beads throughout the loaf, accompanied by a light, fluffy texture. The bread is rich, wholesome and has a lovely appearance. Extra crunch is added by the seed topping, or the loaf can be removed from the pan and baked on the oven rack for an extra 5-8 minutes.

OVEN TIME: 30 minutes at 400 degrees   **YIELD:** 2 loaves

2 cups warm water	3 Tablespoons buttermilk powder
1 Tablespoon Saf yeast	3 Tablespoons millet flour
2 Tablespoons honey	½ cup millet, cooked
2 Tablespoons canola oil	¼ cup walnuts, chopped
2 teaspoons sea salt	⅓ cup sunflower seeds, chopped
2 teaspoons onion flakes	
5½-6 cups all-purpose flour, or bread flour	

In a large bowl or electric mixer bowl, dissolve the yeast in the warm water. Add the honey. Stir to dissolve. Add 2 cups flour. Beat for 2 minutes. Scrape down the inside of the bowl. Add cooked millet and canola oil. Beat 2 minutes.

In a separate bowl, blend the sea salt, onion flakes, walnuts, sunflower seeds, dry buttermilk and millet flour. Gradually add the dry ingredients to the yeast batter. Beat after each addition. Scrape down the inside of the bowl. When the dough begins to climb the dough hook, turn the dough out onto a sprinkling of flour. Knead 6-8 minutes.

Place the dough in an oiled bowl. Turn to coat all sides with oil. Cover. Let rise until doubled in bulk. Knead the dough down. Turn the dough out on a flat surface. Press out the remaining air bubbles. Divide the dough. Let it rest for 6-8 minutes. Form the loaves. Place in oiled, or sprayed pans. Cover. Let rise until nearly doubled in bulk.

Brush with 1 egg white, whisked with 2 Tablespoons of water. Sprinkle with the Quinoa Seed Topping, or your own favorite seed topping. Bake on the middle rack of the oven. When the loaves are finished, remove from the pan. Cool on a rack.

DOUBLE-FERMENT SPELT BREAD

Note: This old-world grain contains gluten, as does wheat, but it is highly soluble, so the nutrients are available to the body. Wheat-sensitive individuals can normally eat spelt without stress. Spelt bread can be baked in automatic bread machines. However, since bread machines are generally programmed for hard winter wheat, spelt breads will demand a bit more attention and experimentation. Spelt loaves have a tendency to rise to optimum height in the machine, but sometimes they deflate slightly toward the end of the baking cycle. It is best to grind the grain a bit finer than usual, if you make your own flour.

OVEN TIME: 30 minutes at 375 degrees   **YIELD:** 2 large loaves

STARTER: See Headstart Sourdough

BREAD RECIPE:

1 cup sourdough starter	½ teaspoon lecithin granules
1½ cups warm water	2 Tablespoons canola oil
2 Tablespoons brown sugar	2 teaspoons sea salt
2 teaspoons Saf yeast	2 Tablespoons soy milk
½ cup evaporated milk	powder or soy flour
	6½-7 cups spelt flour

In a large bowl or an electric mixer bowl, dissolve the yeast in the warm water. Add the brown sugar. Stir to dissolve. Stir in the sourdough. Blend well. Add 2 cups spelt flour. Beat 2 minutes. Scrape down the inside of the bowl. Stir in the milk, lecithin granules, canola oil, sea salt and soy milk powder. Scrape down the inside of the bowl. Gradually add the remaining flour. Beat after each addition.

When the dough begins to climb the dough hook, turn it out on a flat surface onto a sprinkling of flour. Knead well. (This dough is soft and very pliable, due to the variety of flour blends. Do not let that encourage you to add too much flour.) Place the dough in an oiled bowl. Turn to all sides. Cover and let rise until doubled in bulk. Punch down the dough. Turn out on a flat surface. Press out the remaining air bubbles. Divide the dough. Let it rest for 6-8 minutes.

Form the loaves. Place in oiled pans. Cover. Let rise until nearly doubled in bulk. Brush the top of the loaves with oil, if a soft crust is desired. Bake. Remove from the pans. Cool on a rack.

 Yeast Bread

ENGINEHOUSE BREAD

Note: When the fire bell clangs and the firemen slide down the greased pole there is little time to think about a sandwich, but never fear. This quick and easy bread is so flavorful that a chunk of bread can be torn from the loaf, slipped into the pocket and munched en route to the blaze.

OVEN TIME: 30-35 minutes at 400 degrees   **YIELD:** 2 loaves

3 cups warm water	2 teaspoons parsley, minced
1 Tablespoon instant dry yeast	4 teaspoons sea salt
1 cup potato sourdough	2 teaspoons dill weed
3 Tablespoons sugar or honey	½ teaspoon ground sage
3 Tablespoons dry onion flakes	½ cup cornmeal
3 Tablespoons sunflower oil	5 cups unbleached white flour
	4-4½ cups whole wheat flour

In a large bowl or electric mixer bowl, dissolve the yeast in warm water and add the sugar or honey. Let rest until foamy (if time permits). Stir in the sourdough. Beat in 4 cups white flour. Beat 2 minutes. Stop the motor. Let the "sponge" rest until bubbly. In a separate bowl, blend together the onion flakes, parsley, sea salt, dill weed, sage, cornmeal and the remaining flour. Set aside.

Add the oil, stir to blend. Gradually add the remaining dry ingredients. Beat after each addition. Stop the machine and scrape down the inside of the bowl. When the dough begins to leave the sides of the bowl, turn it out onto a sprinkling of flour. Knead 6-8 minutes, or until the dough is smooth and elastic. Place it in an oiled bowl. Turn to coat all sides of the dough. Cover with wax paper and a cloth. Let rise until doubled in bulk.

Punch down. Form the loaves. Place in oiled or sprayed loaf pans. Let rise to near doubled in bulk. Brush with milk if a soft crust is desired. Sprinkle with cornmeal. Bake. When the loaves are finished remove them from the pans. Cool on racks.

"Keep calm; the life of the cells is run by emotions."
Ferne Chapman

EXTRAORDINARY HERB BREAD

Note: The intense flavor for this bread is created by steaming the herbs. Do not boil. These herbs lend a savory flavor to the dough.

OVEN TIME: 35 minutes at 375 Degrees   **YIELD:** 3 loaves

3 cups warm milk	1 egg
¼ cup butter	1 teaspoon ground sage
1 teaspoon sea salt	1 teaspoon ground thyme
¼ cup oatmeal	1 teaspoon marjoram
1 cup warm water	4 cups bread flour.
5 teaspoons instant dry yeast	or unbleached white flour
½ cup Parmesan cheese, grated	6½-7 cups whole wheat flour

In a small saucepan heat the milk and add the herbs. Stir in the butter, sea salt and oatmeal. Remove from the heat. Cool until warm to the touch. In a large bowl or electric mixer bowl, dissolve the yeast in the warm water. Add the sugar. Add the milk mixture. Beat in the white flour. Beat 2 minutes. Scrape down the inside of the bowl. Add the egg and Parmesan cheese. Blend.

In a separate small bowl, combine the remaining dry ingredients. Gradually add them to the batter. Scrape down the inside of the bowl. When the dough leaves the side of the bowl, turn it out onto a sprinkling of flour. Knead until smooth and elastic. Place the dough in an oiled bowl, turn it to coat all sides of the dough with oil. Cover with wax paper and a cloth. Let rise until doubled in bulk.

Turn out on a flat surface. Press out the remaining air bubbles. Form the loaves. Place in prepared pans. Let rise slightly above the pan. Brush with egg white and water mixture. Sprinkle with 2 Tablespoons dry onion flakes. Bake. Remove bread from the pan. Cool on a rack.

This bread can be made even more extraordinary with the substitution of ½ cup of the Pantry Enrichment Mix. Dinner rolls made from this dough furnish a welcome treat for a hungry family, friends, or for gift giving.

FOUR GRAIN BREAD WITH KASSARI CHEESE

Note: The cheese in this bread not only adds flavor and texture to the bread, but it adds extra calcium and several other important minerals and vitamins.

OVEN TIME: 30-35 minutes at 375 degrees   **YIELD:** 3 loaves

¼ cup flax seed	2 Tablespoons instant yeast
⅓ cup sunflower seeds	2 cups unbleached white flour
½ cup rolled oats	2 cups buttermilk
2 Tablespoons cornmeal	¼ cup safflower oil
1 cup dark rye flour	1 Tablespoon sea salt
2 cups whole wheat flour, freshly ground	1½ cups Kassari cheese, grated
½ cup blackstrap molasses	2 Tablespoons whole milk
2 cups warm water	

Grind flax seed, sunflower seeds, and rolled oats together. Add the cornmeal, rye flour and two cups whole wheat flour. Set aside. In an electric mixer bowl, dissolve the yeast in the warm water. Add the molasses. Add the white flour and 1 cup whole wheat flour. Beat for 2 minutes. Scrape down the inside of the bowl. Add buttermilk, safflower oil and sea salt. Add the Kassari cheese.

Combine whole wheat flour and the multigrain mixture. Gradually add it to the yeast batter. Beat after each addition. When the dough begins to climb the dough hook, turn the mass out onto a sprinkling of flour. Knead until the dough is smooth and elastic. Place the dough in an oiled bowl. Turn to coat all sides of the dough with oil. Cover. Let rise until doubled in bulk. Knead the dough down. Turn it out on a flat surface and press out the remaining air bubbles. Let dough rest for ten minutes. (Use a portion if this dough for dinner rolls if desired.)

Form into loaves. Place in oiled or sprayed loaf pans. If round loaves are desired, place them on a baking sheet. Cover. Let rise until nearly doubled in bulk. Brush the tops of the loaves with the milk. Make two diagonal slits across the top. Sprinkle with cornmeal. Bake. When the bread is finished, remove it from the pans. Place the bread on a rack to cool.

Note: As a substitute for the first four ingredients, use 1½ cups of the seven grain enrichment mix. Any cheese of your choice will also make a tasty loaf.

FOUR GRAIN HERB BREAD

Note: The blended grains and multiple natural ingredients add up for a satisfying, substantial healthy loaf.

OVEN TIME: 30 minutes at 400 degrees   **YIELD:** 2 large loaves

2 cups warm water	¼ cup safflower oil
2 teaspoons caraway seed	2 Tablespoons soy powder, or soy flour
1 teaspoon anise seed	
2 Tablespoons dry onion soup mix	¼ teaspoon vitamin C crystals
4 teaspoons instant dry yeast	1 Tablespoon gluten
2 teaspoons sugar or honey	1 cup rye flour
¼ cup blackstrap molasses	¼ cup buckwheat
½ cup evaporated milk	1 cup barley flour
2 eggs	3½-4 cups unbleached white flour

In a small saucepan, heat one cup of the water and sprinkle in the anise seed, caraway seed, and dry onion soup mix. Remove from heat. Set aside. Cool until warm to the touch.

In a large mixing bowl, dissolve yeast in the remaining cup warm water. Add the sugar. Add 2 cups white flour; beat 2 minutes. Stir in the herbal mixture, evaporated milk, molasses, eggs, safflower oil and the vitamin C crystals. Scrape down the inside of the bowl. Blend together the remaining dry ingredients. Gradually add the mixture to the batter. When the dough begins to leave the side of the bowl, turn it out in a sprinkling of flour. Knead until it becomes smooth and elastic. Place the dough in an oiled bowl. Turn to coat all sides. Cover with wax paper and a cloth. Allow bread to rise until doubled in bulk. Punch down. Let rise again.

Form the loaves. Place in sprayed pans. Let rise until doubled in bulk. Using a razor blade or an extremely sharp thin knife, make a shallow slash lengthwise across the loaf. Bake. When the bread is finished, remove it from the pan. For a tender, shiny crust, brush the top with butter, sweet cream, or whole milk. Cool on a rack.

"To believe you cannot do a thing is a way to make it impossible."
Edna Lister

 Yeast Bread

GARLIC CHEESE CASSEROLE BREAD

Note: Batter breads were frequently used in Cottage kitchens because of the no kneading method. Their sparkling rough appearance and texture was typical of our rough country lifestyle.

OVEN TIME: 35-40 minutes at 400 degrees   **YIELD:** 1½ quart-size loaf

1 cup warm water
1 Tablespoon instant dry yeast
2 Tablespoons sugar or honey
1 cup cottage cheese, pureed

½ teaspoon dill weed
¼ teaspoon oregano (optional)
1 clove garlic, minced
2 Tablespoons Blend oil
3 cups unbleached white flour

In a mixer bowl, dissolve the yeast in warm water. Add the sugar. Puree the cottage cheese. Add the cheese, herbs, garlic and oil to the yeast mixture. Add 2 cups flour. Beat 2 minutes. Scrape down the inside of the bowl. Gradually add the remaining flour. If needed, add a little more flour to make a stiff dough. Let the dough rise until doubled in bulk in the same bowl. Stir down.
Spoon the batter into a well-oiled casserole dish (or a prepared loaf pan). Brush with mixture of 1 egg white and 2 Tablespoons water. Sprinkle on dill weed. Let rise again until it barely arches over the container. Bake. Serve hot, cut in pie shape wedges.

There are three basic types of yeast dough for making bread:

1). Water dough for crusty french bread and crusty rolls.

2). Milk dough for richer dough and sweet rolls.

3). Sweet dough for fancy breads differ in liquids and the amount of shortening, sugar and eggs used.

"What you ask for others shall be your portion doubled."
Edna Lister

GRANOLA BATTER BREAD

OVEN TIME: 40 minutes at 350 degrees   **YIELD:** 1 large loaf

4 teaspoons instant
dry yeast
1 Tablespoon brown sugar
½ cup warm water
1 cup milk
2 Tablespoons butter, melted

3 Tablespoons honey
1 teaspoon sea salt
2 eggs
2 cups whole wheat flour
2 cups all-purpose flour
1⅔ cups Grain-Bin Granola

In a large bowl or electric mixer bowl, dissolve the yeast in warm water. Add the brown sugar. Stir to dissolve. Add the milk, butter, honey and sea salt. Stir to blend. Add 3 cups flour. Beat 2 minutes. Scrape down the inside of the bowl. Add the eggs, one at a time, beating after each addition. Add the granola. Gradually add the remaining flour until the dough begins to leave the sides of the bowl. Cover and let rise until nearly doubled. Stir down and spoon unto a generously oiled large loaf pan, or two medium-size pans. Push the dough well into the corners of the pan. Sprinkle granola over the top. Let the batter rise until it forms a slight arch over the top of the pan. Bake. When the loaf is finished, remove it from the pan. Cool on a rack.

Bread

Ideas
are the ingredients
of the bread of life.
Many are the loaves that are brought
to be browned
in the brimming ovens of the brain,
leavend with expectancy,
kneaded with constancy,
crusty with creativity.

Consumed then, the consummation,
and metabolized
in the reality of retrospect.

Mildred Hoffman

GOOD FRIDAY HOT CROSS BUNS

OVEN TIME: 35-40 minutes at 375 degrees   **YIELD:** 30 buns

1 cup raisins or currants	1 Tablespoon lemon juice
1¼ cups water	½ teaspoon allspice
½ cup raw potato	½ teaspoon nutmeg
5 teaspoons instant dry yeast	2 teaspoons cinnamon
½ cup brown sugar	1 teaspoon sea salt
1 cup milk, warm	3 Tablespoons orange zest
½ cup butter, melted	¼ cup soy milk powder
3 eggs	2 cups pastry flour
	5½-6 cups unbleached white flour

Soak the raisins in warm water. Cook ½ cup diced potato in the ¾ cup water. Mash. Remove from the heat. Cool until warm to the touch. In a large bowl or electric mixer bowl, dissolve the yeast in the warm potato water. Add 1 Tablespoon brown sugar. Stir to dissolve. Add 2 cups flour. Beat 2 minutes. Scrape down the inside of the bowl. Add the milk, the remaining brown sugar and butter. Stir beat to blend. Add the eggs, one at a time; beat after each addition. Add the orange zest.

In a separate bowl, blend together the remaining dry ingredients. Gradually add the mixture to the batter. Scrape down the inside of the bowl. When the dough leaves the side of the bowl, turn it out onto a sprinkling of flour. Knead the dough lightly; add only enough flour for easy handling. This is a light, smooth dough.

Place the dough in an oiled bowl. Turn to coat all sides. Cover and let rise until doubled in bulk. Press out the remaining air bubbles. Divide the dough into approximately 2-ounce balls. With oiled palms, mold the buns. Dip the top into a mixture of 1 egg whisked with 2 Tablespoons water. Place them ½ inch apart on an oiled baking sheet. Using a sharp knife or a razor blade, cut a cross in the top of each bun. Cover. Let rise until nearly doubled in bulk. Bake on the middle oven rack. Remove from the pan. Cool on a rack. If desired, decorate the cross with Confectioner's sugar frosting.

> *"If any man will come after me, let him deny himself,*
> *and take up his cross daily, and follow me."*
> *Luke 9:23*

Yeast Bread   41

HARVEST BREAD

Note: For breadmakers, improvisation in the pantry can be one of the your greatest assets. This bread has a spicy, yet unassertive flavor. Extra crustiness can be added after the baking process is completed. See note below.

OVEN TIME: 30-40 minutes at 375 Degrees   **YIELD:** 2 large loaves

3 cups water	2 Tablespoons instant yeast
¼ cup cornmeal	¼ cup dark molasses
¼ cup oatmeal	2 eggs
¼ cup barley flakes	2 teaspoons sea salt
4 teaspoons pizza seasoning	3 Tablespoons safflower oil
2 Tablespoons onion flakes	3 cups unbleached white flour
	5-5½ cups whole wheat flour

Heat 2 cups of water in a medium saucepan. Sprinkle in the cornmeal, oatmeal, barley flakes, pizza seasoning and onion flakes. Remove from the heat. Cool until warm to the touch.

In an electric mixer bowl, dissolve the yeast in the remaining warm water. Add the molasses and blend. Add the white flour. Beat 2 minutes. Scrape down the inside of the bowl. Add the oatmeal mixture, sea salt and the safflower oil. Beat to blend. Scrape down the inside of the bowl. Add the eggs, one at a time. Beat after each addition. Gradually add the remaining flour. Knead the dough until it is smooth and elastic. Place the dough in an oiled bowl. Turn to coat all sides with oil. Cover. Let rise until doubled in bulk.

Punch the dough down. Turn out on a flat surface. Press out the remaining air bubbles. Divide the dough into equal portions. Form the loaves. Place in oiled baking pans. Let rise to nearly doubled in bulk. If desired, brush the tops with 1 egg white, whisked with 2 Tablespoons of water. Sprinkle with the seed topping. Bake. Remove from the pans. Cool on a rack.

Note: Making a heavier crust: while the bread is still hot, remove the loaf from the pan and place it on the oven rack. Bake at 450 degrees for 5-8 minutes. Remove and serve. Your friends will enjoy eating the "snap, crackle and pop" crust.

  Yeast Bread

HAWAIIAN DELIGHT BREAD

This bread allows you to utilize leftover bits of home canned fruits, or the Sunday brunch fruit salad. The bread is fluffy, snow white and delightfully delicious. This bread will bake beautifully in a La Cloche. (A stoneware pan with a dome lid.)

OVEN TIME: 30 minutes at 400 degrees   **YIELD:** 2 loaves

1 cup milk, scalded	1 Tablespoon honey
2 Tablespoons butter	¼ cup soy milk powder
½ teaspoon sea salt	⅓ cup coconut, soaked, drained
¼ cup pear juice	¼ cup pineapple juice
2 canned pear halves	1 Tablespoon lemon juice
1 Tablespoon instant dry yeast	¼ cup soy flour
2 pineapple slices, diced, or ⅓ cup crushed, drained	5½-6 cups unbleached white flour

In a small saucepan heat the milk; add the butter and sea salt. Remove from the heat. Puree the pears in the pear juice and add to the milk.

In a large bowl or electric mixer bowl, dissolve the yeast in the warm mixture; add the honey. Add 3 cups of flour. Beat 2 minutes. Turn off the motor. Scrape down the side of the bowl. Add the pineapple, pineapple juice, lemon juice and coconut. Beat. Blend the soy milk powder and soy flour with 1 cup of flour; add it to the batter. Gradually add the remaining flour. Beat after each addition. Scrape down the inside of the bowl.

When the dough begins to climb the dough hook, turn it out on a flat surface onto a sprinkling of flour. Knead until smooth and elastic. Place the dough in an oiled bowl. Turn the dough to coat all sides. Cover with wax paper and a cloth. Let rise until doubled in bulk.

Punch the dough down. Turn it out on a flat surface and press out the remaining air bubbles. Divide the dough. Form the loaves. Place in greased pans. Cover and let rise until slightly above the top of the pan. Brush the top of the loaves with oil, if desired. Bake. When the loaves are finished, cool on a rack.

"Resolve to keep happy and your joy shall form a sheild against difficulty"
Edna Lister

HERITAGE BREAD

Note: Cereal grains are a part of our heritage. They have returned to our diets from processed breakfast cereals-as integral ingredients for making wholesome breads. This bread will furnish plenty of nutrients for the brown bagger's lunch.

OVEN TIME: 30-35 minutes at 375 degrees   **YIELD:** 2 large loaves

2 cups warm water	2 Tablespoons flax seed
5 teaspoons instant dry yeast	2 Tablespoons gluten
3 Tablespoons honey	4 cups whole wheat flour
2 Tablespoons molasses	3 cups unbleached white flour
1 cup milk	1 egg white whisked,
2 Tablespoons butter	with 2 Tablespoons water
2 teaspoons sea salt	

In a small sauce pan, cook 3 Tablespoons of cracked rye, or cracked wheat, 2 Tablespoons millet and 2 Tablespoons cornmeal in 1 cup of the water. Simmer 5 minutes. Remove from the heat. Stir in the butter, the molasses, 2 Tablespoons of the honey and the milk.

In a large bowl or electric mixer bowl. Dissolve the yeast in the remaining cup of warm water. Add the remaining honey. If time allows, let rest until foamy. Add 2 cups of flour. Beat for 2 minutes. Add the cooked cereal. Beat 2 minutes. Blend the remaining dry ingredients together. Gradually add them to the batter. When the dough begins to leave the side of the bowl, turn it out onto a sprinkling of flour. Knead 5-6 minutes, until the dough is smooth and elastic.

Place the dough in an oiled bowl. Turn to coat all sides. Cover and let rest for 10-20 minutes. Press out the air bubbles. Place in prepared loaf pans.

Let rise until doubled in bulk. Bake. When the loaves are finished, remove them from the pans. Cool on a wire rack.

Here's a better method for whole grain breadmaking than above. Let the dough rise twice. Punch down after each rising period. Turn out and press out the remaining air bubbles. Form the loaves. Brush tops lightly with egg white whisked in water. Bake.

NOTE: The extra rising period will not only make a lighter textured loaf, but the yeast action has more time to break down harmful phytates in the whole grain. This bread will brown rapidly due to the presence of the extra grains. Enrichment Mix may be substituted for the rye, millet and cornmeal.

JALAPENO PEPPER CHEESE BREAD

This pungent loaf not only makes a good sandwich, but it is a hot conversation piece. Serve hot with butter and honey.

OVEN TIME: 35-40 minutes at 375 degrees   **YIELD:** 1 loaf

2 cups warm water, or potato water	1 teaspoon sea salt
2½ teaspoons Saf yeast	¼ cup Enrichment Mix
2 teaspoons sugar or honey	¼ cup Parmesan cheese, grated
⅛ teaspoon red pepper flakes	2 cups whole wheat flour
2 Tablespoons butter, melted	4½-5 cups high-gluten flour
½ cup tomato sauce	4-6 lengths Pepper Cheese, or Sharp Cheddar cheese, 4 x 2 inches
2 Tablespoons soy milk powder or soy flour	

In a large bowl or electric mixer bowl, dissolve the yeast in the warm potato water. Add the sugar, or honey. Let the mixture rest until foamy. Add 4 cups high-gluten flour. Beat 2 minutes. Add the butter, pepper flakes and tomato sauce. Blend. Scrape down the inside of the bowl. In a separate bowl, blend the remaining flour with the soy milk, sea salt, Enrichment Mix and the Parmesan cheese. Gradually add it to the batter. Beat. When the dough leaves the side of the bowl, turn it out onto a sprinkling of flour. Knead until the dough is smooth and elastic. Make a ball of the dough and place it in an oiled bowl. Turn to coat all sides.

Cover and let rise until doubled in bulk.
Punch down. Turn it out and press out the remaining air bubbles. Flatten the dough with your palms. Arrange the cheese strips a few inches apart in the center of the loaf. Form a round dome of the dough (or bake in 2 smaller loaf pans). Place in a well-oiled pan. Let rise until nearly doubled in bulk.

Brush with an egg white and water mixture. Sprinkle with sunflower seeds, oatmeal, or sesame seeds. Bake. When the loaf is finished, remove it from the pan. Cool on a rack.

Note: Bread that contains milk, or a few teaspoons of applesauce, as a rule will brown more quickly and retain moisture longer.

LIGHT RYE BREAD

Note: This bread is made with white rye flour and additional soaked dark rye flakes. The rye flakes enhance both the texture and the nutritional value of the bread. Oatmeal, triticale or barley flakes may be substituted for the rye.

OVEN TIME: 35 minutes at 375 degrees   **YIELD:** 2 loaves

1 cup potato water	2 Tablespoons onion flakes
1/3 cup rye flakes	1 Tablespoon flax seed
1 cup buttermilk	2 teaspoons fennel seed
4 teaspoons Saf yeast, or Red Star active yeast	3 Tablespoons blended oil
2 Tablespoons honey	1½ cups white bread flour
1½ teaspoons sea salt	2 cups whole wheat flour
	2 cups white rye flour

Soak the rye flakes in ½ cup potato water for 20 minutes. Set aside. Dissolve the yeast in the remaining warm water. Add it to a large bowl or electric mixer bowl; add the honey. If time allows, let the mixture rest until bubbly. Add the buttermilk and the soaked mixture. Stir in the flour and 1 cup of whole wheat flour . Beat for 2 minutes. Add the sea salt, onion flakes, flax seed, fennel and oil. Beat 2 minutes. In a small bowl blend together the remaining whole wheat flour and white rye flour. Gradually add the mixture to the batter.

Scrape down the inside of the bowl. When dough begins to pull away from the sides of the bowl, turn it out in a sprinkling of flour. Knead until the dough becomes smooth and elastic. Shape it into a ball. Place in an oiled bowl. Turn to coat all sides with oil. Cover with wax paper and a cloth. Let rise until doubled in bulk.

Punch down. (If time allows, let it rise again.) Turn the dough out on a flat surface. Press out the remaining air bubbles. Divide the dough. Let it rest for 10 minutes. Form the loaves. Place in oiled pans on a sprinkling of cornmeal. Let rise until nearly doubled in bulk. Brush with the egg white and water mixture. Sprinkle with cracked rye berries, corn meal, or sunflower seeds. Slit a pattern in the top if desired. Bake in round-free-form style or in French-style loaves.

> *"The minute man was given the faculty of reason, he laid aside common sense."*
> Edna Lister

LYNN'S WHOLE GRAIN BREAD

Note: This recipe makes an excellent practice dough for the novice bread-maker. Once you learn the fundamentals of making simple breads, you'll be baking for the sheer joy of handling this smooth, elastic dough. Bread-making time can become "play dough" time for the children, while they learn how to mix good bread.

OVEN TIME: 30-35 minutes at 375 degrees   **YIELD:** 4 loaves

3 cups milk, scalded	2 Tablespoons dry onion flakes
1½ cups potato water	2 Tablespoons soy flour
2 Tablespoons instant dry yeast	4 teaspoons sea salt
2 Tablespoons honey or sugar	5 cups bread flour, or unbleached white flour
¼ cup dark molasses	6-6½ cups whole wheat flour
2 Tablespoons Italian herb mix	3 Tablespoons nutritional yeast, (optional)
3 Tablespoons canola oil	
2 Tablespoons gluten	

In a small saucepan scald the milk. Remove from heat. Cool until warm to the touch. In a large bowl or electric mixer bowl, dissolve the yeast in the potato water and add the sugar. Let rest until foamy. Beat in 2 cups of white flour. Beat 2 minutes. Add the molasses and milk. Stir to blend. Add the sea salt, canola oil, herb mix and dry onion flakes. Beat to blend.

In a separate bowl, blend the gluten, soy flour and nutritional yeast with 1 cup of bread flour. Gradually add it to the sponge. Beat 2 minutes. When the dough begins to leave the sides of the bowl, turn it out in a sprinkling of flour. Knead well. Place the dough in an oiled bowl and turn to coat all sides. Cover and let rise until doubled in bulk. Punch down. Turn out on a flat surface. Press out the remaining air bubbles. Divide the dough. Let it rest for 6-8 minutes. Form the loaves. Place in oiled pans. Cover and let rise until nearly doubled. Bake. When the loaves are finished, remove them from the pans. Cool on a rack.

"Earn your pearls the hard way. Work for them."
Linda Mahalic

MILLET MULTIGRAIN BREAD

Note: We farm children called this aromatic bread "chicken scratch" bread because the mixture of grains and seeds closely resembled the early morning "scatter" used for the chickens. The nutty, whole-grain flavor "eeks" through this off-white, feather-light loaf. Don't worry—your wings will not flap like chicken wings if you eat it! The bread is rich, filling, wholesome and has a "bunch o' crunch."

OVEN TIME: 30-35 minutes at 375 degrees   **YIELD:** 2 loaves

1	cup warm water	⅓	cup millet flour
2	teaspoons Saf yeast	1	Tablespoon pizza seasoning
2	Tablespoons honey	1	cup Pantry Enrichment Mix
½	cup cooked millet	¼	cup walnuts, chopped
¾	cup whole milk	2	teaspoons sea salt
3	Tablespoons sunflower seed oil	2½	cups all-purpose flour
		2	cups whole wheat flour

In a large bowl or electric mixer bowl, dissolve the yeast in the warm water. Add the honey. Stir to dissolve. Add 2 cups flour. Beat 2 minutes. Scrape down the inside of the bowl. Add the milk, cooked millet and sunflower seed oil. Beat to blend.

In a separate bowl, stir together the pizza seasoning, Enrichment Mix, sea salt and the remaining flour. Gradually add the mixture to the batter. Beat after each addition. Scrape down the inside of the bowl. When the dough begins to clean the bowl, turn it out onto a sprinkling of flour. Knead 6-8 minutes, or until the dough is smooth and elastic. Place the dough in an oiled bowl. Turn to coat all sides of the dough. Cover and let rise until doubled in bulk.

Knead the dough down. Turn it out on a flat surface. Press out the remaining air bubbles. Divide the dough and let it rest for 6-8 minutes. Form the loaves. Place in greased pans. Cover and let rise until nearly doubled in bulk. Brush the top with 1 egg white whisked in 2 teaspoons water. Sprinkle with Quinoa Seed Topping, or your own favorite topping. Bake. Remove the bread from the pans. Cool on a rack.

"Doubt is a necessary tool for gaining knowledge."
Ferne Chapman

MILLET SAFFRON BREAD

Note: This golden loaf is by far the smoothest, most colorful and tasty bread that one could imagine. Its appearance and flavor is only surpassed by the dough's superior handling quality.

OVEN TIME: 30 minutes at 400 degrees   **YIELD:** 2 loaves

1 cup water	1 cup Enrichment Mix
1 small potato, scrubbed, diced	¾ teaspoon saffron
1 cup warm milk	1 egg
1 Tablespoon instant dry yeast	1 teaspoon sea salt
3 Tablespoons honey	¼ cup quick oatmeal
⅓ cup millet, cooked	2 Tablespoons gluten
	5½-6 cups unbleached white flour, or whole wheat flour

In a small saucepan cook the potato in 1 cup water. Mash it in the cooking water. Remove it from the heat. Cool until warm to the touch. In a large bowl or electric mixer bowl, dissolve the yeast in the warm milk; add the honey. Add 2 cups flour. Beat for 2 minutes. Scrape the inside of the bowl. Add the potato water, millet, and egg. Beat one minute.

In a separate bowl, blend the remaining flour, Enrichment Mix, saffron, quick oatmeal, gluten and sea salt. Gradually add the dry ingredients. Beat after each addition. Scrape down the inside of the bowl. When the dough begins to climb the dough hook, turn it out on a flat surface onto a sprinkling of flour. Knead well. Place the dough in an oiled bowl. Turn to coat all sides of the dough. Cover and let rise until doubled in bulk.

Punch the dough down. Turn it out on a flat surface and press out the remaining air bubbles. Divide the dough. Let it rest for 6-8 minutes. Form the loaves. Place in sprayed pans. Cover and let rise until nearly doubled. Brush the top of the loaves with 1 egg white whisked with 1 Tablespoon water. Bake. When the loaves are finished; remove from the pans. Cool on a rack.

NOTE: Millet is cooked the same way as rice. Bring the water to a rolling boil. Sprinkle the millet into the water slowly. Stir once. Lower the heat. Cover and simmer until near done. Save cooking time by preparing a larger amount than needed and freezing the remainder. Millet makes an excellent breakfast cereal and pudding. (4 cups water to ½-⅔ cup millet will yield a semi-dry millet curd.) For breakfast cereal, add raisins, apple, figs or dates. Warm the millet in milk.

OAT BERRY BREAD

Note: Modern scientific research reports that oat products, vitamin C and high density cholesterol have an affinity for each other. If that is the case, this bread could be more valuable than we first thought. This loaf is winner for fiber content and taste. It is a perfect lunch box food.

OVEN TIME: 30-35 minutes at 375 degrees   **YIELD:** 3 loaves

⅓ cup oat berries	1 cup warm water
⅔ cup water	2 Tablespoons brown sugar
2 cups milk, scalded	¼ cup dark molasses
1½ cups oat flakes	¼ cup Enrichment Mix
3 Tablespoons oat bran	5 cups unbleached white flour
¼ cup butter	3½-4 cups whole wheat flour
2 teaspoons sea salt	1 egg white
2 Tablespoons instant dry yeast	2 Tablespoons water

Steam the oat berries in ⅔ cup water, or sprout the berries three days prior to making the bread. Scald the milk and pour over the oat flakes, oat bran, butter and sea salt. Stir to blend. Cool until warm to the touch.

In a large bowl, dissolve the yeast in the cup of warm water. Add the brown sugar and molasses. Add the oat berries mix. Add 3 cups white flour. Beat 2 minutes. Scrape down the inside of the bowl. Mix together the remaining flour and the Enrichment Mix. Slowly add it to the batter. Beat after each addition. When the dough begins to leave the side of the bowl, turn it out in a sprinkling of flour. Knead until the dough is smooth and elastic. This dough will be a bit tacky due to the ingredients. Place the dough in an oiled bowl, turn to coat all sides with oil. Cover with wax paper and a cloth. Let rise until doubled in bulk.

Press out the remaining air bubbles. Divide the dough. Let rest for 5 minutes. Form the loaves. Place in oiled, or sprayed pans. Let rise until nearly doubled. Brush with the egg white mixture. Sprinkle with Seed Topping. Bake. Remove from the pans. Cool on a rack.

"Somewhere on the back burner of our soul, there is something going on, lets find out what that is."
David Mahalic

OATMEAL BRAN BREAD

OVEN TIME: 40 minutes at 375 degrees   **YIELD:** 3 large loaves

3 cups boiling water	¼ cup honey
2 cups rolled oats	3 Tablespoons dark molasses
¼ cup nonfat dry milk	¼ cup Miller's bran
¼ cup safflower oil	2 Tablespoons gluten
1 Tablespoon sea salt	2 Tablespoons wheat germ
1 cup warm water	1 Tablespoon Dough
2 Tablespoons	Enhancer, optional
instant dry yeast	6½-7 cups bread flour

In a large bowl or an electric mixer bowl, stir together the first 5 ingredients. Cool until warm to the touch. Add the molasses to the oatmeal mixture. Dissolve the yeast in 1 cup warm water and add the honey. Let rest until foamy. Stir the yeast into the oatmeal mixture.

In a separate bowl blend together the bran, gluten, wheat germ, Dough Enhancer and 3 cups flour. Gradually add it to the oatmeal/yeast. Beat 2 minutes. Add the remaining flour, one cup at a time, beating after each addition. Scrape down the inside of the bowl at intervals. When the dough begins to leave the sides of the bowl, turn it out in a sprinkling of flour. Knead until the dough is smooth and elastic. Place the dough in an oiled bowl. Turn oiled side up. Cover and let rise until doubled in bulk.

Punch down. Form the loaves and place in greased pans. Let rise slightly over the pan. Bake. Cool on a rack.

For All Types of Dough Decorating
Roll the dough very thin, cut with a variety of tiny cookie cutters. Glaze the loaf and scatter the cut-outs around the loaf.

Roll the dough very thin. Form a lattice-work crown over the top, as if covering a pie.

OATMEAL CHEDDAR BREAD

Note: In these times of synthetic flavorings and overly processed foods, it is both refreshing and healthful to select wholesome food substances and herbs which add a subtle and truly distinctive taste to the loaf of bread.

OVEN TIME: 35 minutes at 400 degrees   **YIELD:** 2 large loaves

1½	cups water	½	teaspoon dried marjoram
½	cup oatmeal	⅓	cup Enrichment Mix
¼	cup butter	1¼	cups sharp cheddar cheese, grated
2	teaspoons sea salt		
1½	cups milk	4	cups unbleached white flour or bread flour
5	teaspoons instant dry yeast		
3	Tablespoons honey	2½-3	cups whole wheat pastry flour
1	teaspoon each, fresh thyme, sage, minced		

In a medium saucepan heat the water; stir in the oatmeal, butter and sea salt. Set aside. Cool until warm to the touch.

In a large mixing bowl or electric mixer bowl, dissolve the yeast in the warm oatmeal mixture. Add the milk and honey. If time permits, let rest for 10 minutes. Stir in 2 cups of the white flour. Beat 2 minutes.

Scrape down the inside of the bowl. Add the herbs, Enrichment Mix and 1 cup of the cheddar cheese. Stir lightly to blend. Stir together the remaining flour. Add it to the batter. Beat 2 minutes. When the dough begins to leave the side of the bowl, turn it out onto a sprinkling of flour. Knead for 6-8 minutes, or until the dough is smooth and elastic.

Place the dough in an oiled bowl, turn to coat all sides of the dough with oil. Cover with wax paper and a cloth. Let rise until doubled in bulk. Turn the dough out; press out the remaining air bubbles. Knead lightly.
Divide the dough. Form the loaves. Placed in greased loaf pans. Let rise until doubled in bulk. Brush tops lightly with egg white whisked into 2 Tablespoons water. Sprinkle with coarsely ground oatmeal, if desired.
Bake. When the loaves are finished, remove from the pan. Cool on a rack.

  Yeast Bread

OLD MILL APPLE NUT BREAD

Note: Dollar for dollar you get more protein out of oatmeal than from any other commonly used cereal grain food item. Oatmeal is rich in calcium, iron and several of the vitamin B-Complex family. It is one of the high-fiber foods needed by most people.

OVEN TIME: 35 minutes at 375 Degrees   **YIELD:** 4 loaves

2	cups boiling water	¼	cup dark molasses
¼	cup oat bran	1	Tablespoon lemon juice
1	cup oatmeal	1½	Tablespoons sea salt
¼	cup butter	½	cup Pantry Enrichment mix
1	small apple, peeled, diced	1	cup walnuts, chopped
2	cups warm water	4	cups unbleached white flour
2	Tablespoons instant yeast	6-6½	cups whole wheat flour
2	Tablespoons sugar or honey		

Heat the water in a medium saucepan. Sprinkle in the oat bran, oatmeal, and add the butter and apple. Remove from the heat. Cool until warm to the touch. In an electric mixer bowl, dissolve the yeast in the warm water. Add the sugar. Add 3 cups white flour. Beat 2 minutes. Scrape down the inside of the bowl. Add the oatmeal mixture. Beat well. Add the molasses and the lemon juice. Beat to blend. Scrape down the inside of the bowl. In a separate small bowl, blend the sea salt, Pantry Enrichment mix and the remaining flour.

Gradually add it to the batter. Beat well. When the dough leaves the side of the bowl, turn it out onto a sprinkling of flour. Knead until the dough is smooth and elastic. Place the dough in an oiled bowl. Turn to coat all sides with oil. Cover. Let rise until doubled in bulk. Punch the dough down. Turn out on a flat surface. Press out the remaining air bubbles. Divide the dough into equal portions. Form the loaves. Place in oiled baking pans. Let rise until nearly doubled in bulk.

Brush the tops with 1 egg white, whisked with 2 Tablespoons water. Sprinkle with the seed topping. Bake. When the loaves are finished, remove from the pans. Cool on a rack.

NOTE: If the Pantry Enrichment is not used, add ¼ cup of soy flour and ¼ cup more of either the whole wheat or white flour.

100 PERCENT WHOLE WHEAT BREAD

Note: This bread is mixed using a so-called quick method. Note the water temperature. The water must be 120-130 degrees Fahrenheit and can be finished in about one-half the time when gluten is beaten into the mixture by using the electric mixer. One rising is all that is needed with this method because the mixer incorporates ample air into the dough. This dough is excellent for hamburger buns. Expect a fine smooth texture with plenty of flavor.

OVEN TIME: 30-35 minutes at 350 degrees   **YIELD:** 2 loaves
              20 minutes at 350 degrees   6 buns

7-7½ cups freshly ground whole wheat flour	1 teaspoon herbal seasoning mix
2 cups hot water (120°)	2 teaspoons sea salt
1 cup warm milk	¼ cup polyunsaturated oil
⅓ cup honey	1 egg white
2 Tablespoons dry yeast	1 Tablespoon water
2 Tablespoons Dough Enhancer, (optional)	

Add the hot water and warm milk to a large bowl or electric mixer bowl. Beat in the honey and 2 cups of flour. Beat for 2 minutes. Add the yeast. Beat 2 minutes. Blend the Dough Enhancer, seasoning mix and salt, with 2 cups of flour. Add it to the batter. Beat 2 minutes.

Gradually add the remaining flour. When the dough begins to leave the side of the bowl, turn it out onto a sprinkling of flour. Knead 5-6 minutes, until the dough is smooth and elastic. Place in an oiled bowl. Turn to coat all sides. Cover and let rest for 10-20 minutes.

Press out the air bubbles. Form into loaves. To make hamburger buns, roll the dough to ½-¾ inch thick. Using a 3½ inch cookie cutter, cut desired amount of buns. Place loaves of bread in prepared loaf pans or round baking pans. Let rise until doubled in bulk. Brush tops lightly with egg white whisked in the water. Bake. Cool on a wire rack.

NOTE: For sandwich-size loaves, form dough into two large loaves. For bread sticks, roll small pieces of dough between the palms to the desired length. Let rise. Brush with egg white mixture. Sprinkle with sesame seeds, poppy seeds, or cracked meal. Bake until browned. Cool on a rack.

"Look for opportunity, not guarantees." Edna Lister

PIONEER BREAD

Note: The grain used in this bread is not ground as coarsely as it may have been during the pioneering days; however the bread is scrumptiously delicious, browns very well, and it is chock full of health-building nutrients.

OVEN TIME: 30-35 minutes at 375 degrees   **YIELD:** 2 large loaves

2 cups warm potato water	2 Tablespoons blended oil
5 teaspoons instant dry yeast	2 teaspoons sea salt
3 Tablespoons honey	½ cup Pioneer Enrichment Mix
2 Tablespoons molasses	3 cups unbleached white flour
1 cup milk	4-4½ cups whole wheat flour

Heat the milk to the scald stage. Remove from the heat. Cool until warm to the touch.

In a large bowl or electric mixer bowl, dissolve the yeast in the warm potato water and add the honey. Let rest until foamy, if time allows. Add 2 cups of flour. Beat for 2 minutes. Add the milk and Pioneer Enrichment. Beat 2 minutes. Add the blended oil and sea salt. Stir to blend. Gradually add the remaining flour. When the dough begins to leave the side of the bowl, turn it out onto a sprinkling of flour. Knead 5-6 minutes, until the dough is smooth and elastic. Place in an oiled bowl. Turn to coat all sides. Cover and let rest for 10-20 minutes.

Press out the air bubbles. Place in prepared loaf pans and let rise until doubled in bulk. Brush tops lightly with egg white whisked in water. Bake. When the loaves are finished, remove them from the pans. Cool on a wire rack.

Note: This bread browns rapidly due to the extra grains and soy products in the Pioneer mix.

"You are happy in direct proportion to your efforts in trying to make others happy and yourself good."
Edna Lister

PIZZA BREAD

Note: This bread mix will make a simple good pizza. For those who are health conscious, add ½ cup of the Pantry Enrichment Mix in place of ½ cup of bread flour.

OVEN TIME: 30 minutes at 400 degrees   **YIELD:** 2 pizzas

2 cups Yeast Bread Mix	1 teaspoon ground sage or
1 cup warm water	pizza seasoning
1 egg	2½ cups bread flour
1½ Tablespoon oil	
or lecithin butter	

Stir and measure the flour into a large bowl. In a small bowl, beat together the egg, water and oil. Blend all ingredients together. Knead well. Divide the dough. Cover with a cloth and let it rest for 10 minutes. Roll to size. (Refrigerate, freeze or prepare immediately.) Bring the dough to room temperature before making the pizza.

PIZZA FILLING

1 16 ounce can tomato sauce	6-8 ounces thinly sliced salami
½ pound mushrooms, sliced	4-5 slices purple onion
1 cup ripe black olives, sliced	3 slices of red or green
2 teaspoons parsley, minced	sweet bell pepper
2 cups Mozzarella cheese, grated	

Heat the oven to 400 degrees. Roll the pizza crusts and slightly flute the edges. Add a sprinkling of cheese. Spoon the tomato sauce over the cheese. Add the remaining ingredients in layers. Sprinkle on cheese, salami, peppers, onions, and the remaining cheese and olives.

FILLING ALTERNATIVES

Canadian Bacon, thinly sliced
Pre-browned sausage, smoked
thinly sliced
Ground turkey or lean beef,
sauteed, drained

pineapple chunks, or thin slices
vegetables of your choice
lightly cooked or fresh

For a Deep-Dish Pizza, crusts can be made with whole grain flour, filled with other cheeses (such as a mixture of cottage cheese), and shredded sharp cheddar cheese. Top with fresh tomatoes, dots of cream cheese or tofu squares.

RAISIN RYE WALNUT DOME

Note: This rye loaf has character, flavor and it is a dense loaf. Capped with slashes, popped amaranth and a scatter of sunflower seeds, it resembles an eruption.

OVEN TIME: 10 minutes at 400 degrees
30-35 minutes at 375 degrees   **YIELD:** 1 Large Dome Loaf

1 cup water	3 teaspoons Saf yeast
¼ cup rye flakes	1 teaspoon sugar
1 Tablespoon butter	1 Tablespoon cornmeal
1 teaspoon sea salt	2 cups unbleached white flour
¼ cup molasses	1 cup whole wheat flour
1 Tablespoon fennel seeds	2 cups rye flour
1 cup buttermilk	⅓ cup raisins
¼ cup warm water	⅓ cup walnuts, chopped

In a small saucepan, bring the water to a boil. Sprinkle in the rye flakes and add the butter, sea salt, molasses and fennel seeds. Remove from the heat and set aside.

In a large bowl or electric mixer bowl, dissolve the yeast in warm water and add the sugar. Add the buttermilk. Add 2 cups white flour. Beat 2 minutes. Add the rye mixture. Beat to blend. Scrape down the inside of the bowl.

In a separate bowl blend together the remaining dry ingredients. Gradually add them to the batter. When the dough begins to leave the side of the bowl, turn it out onto a sprinkling of flour. Sprinkle the raisins and nuts over the dough and knead to distribute evenly. Knead until the dough is smooth and elastic. Place it in an oiled bowl, turn to oil all sides. Cover with wax paper and a cloth. Let rise until doubled in bulk.

Punch the dough down. Let rise again, if time permits. Let the dough rest for 5-10 minutes. Form the loaf. Place in prepared round pan, which has been dusted with cornmeal. With a sharp knife cut a slash in the top, if desired. Cover and let rise until nearly doubled in bulk. Brush with egg white whisked in water. Bake. When the loaf is finished, remove it from the pan. Cool on a rack.

RYE AND CHEDDAR BAGUETTE ROLL-UPS

Note: The flavor, texture and unique form of these baguettes is enough to spur anyone into baking daily.

OVEN TIME: 30 minutes at 400 degrees **YIELD:** 2 baguettes

1 cup milk, scalded	2 Tablespoons honey
1½ Tablespoons butter	1 Tablespoon instant yeast
½ teaspoon Atlantic Salt	2½ cups rye flour
⅓ cup rye flakes	2 Tablespoons soy flour
1 cup warm water	2¼ cups all-purpose flour
	5-10 Cheddar sticks or grated cheese

In a small saucepan, scald the milk. Stir in the rye flakes, butter and salt. Remove from the heat and cool until warm to the touch. In a large bowl or electric mixer bowl, dissolve yeast in the warm water. Add the honey and, if time allows, let rest until bubbly. Add 2 cups bread flour. Beat 2 minutes. Add the rye flakes mixture and beat well. Scrape down the inside of the bowl.

In a separate bowl blend the soy flour with the remaining flour. Gradually add it to the batter. Beat after each addition. Stop the motor and scrape down the side of the bowl. When dough begins to pull away from the sides of the bowl, turn dough out onto a sprinkling of flour. Knead until the dough becomes smooth and elastic. Shape dough into a ball. Place in an oiled bowl. Turn to coat all sides of the dough. Cover with wax paper and a cloth.

Let rise in a warm place until doubled in bulk. Punch down. Turn out on a flat surface. Press out air bubbles. Divide the dough, let rest for 10 minutes. Flatten the dough to the length desired. Arrange several (3 to 5) 1½-inch x 2½ inch sticks of cheese inside the loaf. Roll the loaf and seal the edges. Place the seam side down in a sprayed baguette pan. Let rise until doubled in bulk. Brush with the egg white mixture. Sprinkle with cracked rye berries, seeds, or cornmeal, if desired.
NOTE: The addition of soy flour heightens the protein value of the loaf. Soy products and cereals also help baked goods retain moisture.

"Any miracle, speedy or slow, is the result of much previous thinking about it and planning for it."
Edna Lister

 Yeast Bread

SAM CHAPMAN'S AFTER THE GAME SANDWICH

Note: The name Philadelphia means many things to many people. To some it means the place where the first white settlers settled in the 1640's. To others it means home. To the Christian it may mean an awakening of brotherly love in man. Yet to sports fans it is the home of the Philadelphia Phillies. To my grandson Brandon it means Hero, just because Sam was a big leaguer of the Philadelphia Athletics.

OVEN TIME: 35-45 minutes at 375 degrees

YIELD: 3-16 inch braided loaves

2	cups milk	1½	Tablespoons instant yeast
⅓	cup rolled oats	3	Tablespoons sugar or honey
3	Tablespoons butter	½	cup light sour cream
2	teaspoons sea salt	⅔	cup Parmesan cheese
1	Tablespoon pizza seasoning	2	Tablespoons gluten
1	cup warm water	9-9½	cups bread flour
1	egg white	1	Tablespoon water

FILLING:

8	ounces Philadelphia cream cheese	3	Tablespoons green peppers, diced
⅓	cup light sour cream	3-4	Italian tomatoes, thinly sliced
½	cup onion, diced		
3	Tablespoons red pepper, diced	2½	cups salami, julienned
3-3½	cups Havarti cheese, grated	2½	cups cooked ham, julienned

Scald the milk and stir in the next 4 ingredients. Remove from heat and cool until warm to the touch. Meanwhile, dissolve the yeast in warm water. Add the sugar or honey. Let the yeast mixture rest until foamy. Stir in the milk mixture along with the sour cream. In a separate bowl stir the gluten into 4 cups of flour. Add it to the yeast mixture, one cup at a time, beating after each addition. If using an electric mixer, beat 2 minutes with the flat beater. Stop the motor and scrape down the inside of the bowl. Let the sponge rest for 5 minutes or until bubbly. Insert the dough hook; add the Parmesan cheese and beat in the remainder of the flour, one cup at a time. When the dough begins to leave the sides of the bowl, turn the mixture out onto a sprinkling of flour. Knead 8-10 minutes until the dough is smooth and elastic.

Place the dough in an oiled bowl. Turn the oiled side up. Cover with wax paper and a cloth. Let raise until doubled in bulk. Knead down. Let rise again.

Turn out on a flat surface and press out the air bubbles. Divide the dough in half. Roll each half into a ½ inch thick rectangle, 8x16-inches. With the rolling pin, press lightly, making a slight indentation down the center to accommodate the filling. In a small bowl, blend the cream cheese, sour cream and peppers. Spread half the mixture in the well. Begin layering the filling. First a layer of salami, a layer of Havarti cheese, ham and a few dollops of cream cheese mixture and sliced tomato. Using a plastic pizza cutter, cut slantwise 1-inch strips on the outsides of the rectangle, almost to the filling. Begin the braid by pulling the first end strip diagonally across the filling. Bring the opposite strip down across the first strip, leaving no end protruding out the side of the loaf. Braid to the end and seal by pinching the dough together and fold under. Using two large spatulas, gently lift the loaf on to a baking sheet. Let rise until doubled in bulk. Brush with the egg white mixture. Bake until done. Cool on a rack.

Yeast Bread

SESAME SEED BREAD

Note: Americans are responding to the idea that whole foods are important for better health and stamina. This bread, using sesame seeds, is deliciously healthful.

OVEN TIME: 30-35 minutes at 375 degrees   YIELD: 2 loaves

2½ cups potato water	1 teaspoon sea salt
2½ teaspoons instant yeast	2 Tablespoons sesame oil
¼ cup honey	⅔ cup soy flour
1 teaspoon sugar	3 cups high-protein flour
2 eggs	5 cups whole wheat flour
1 cup sesame seed meal	

In a large bowl or electric mixer bowl, dissolve the yeast in ½ cup of the warm potato water. Add the sugar. Let rest until foamy. Add the remaining warm potato water and the white flour, plus 1 cup whole wheat flour. Beat 2 minutes. Scrape down the inside of the bowl. If time allows, let the batter rest for 20 minutes. (This procedure is known as the sponge method for making bread.) Add the sesame oil and the honey. Blend well. Add the eggs, one at a time. Beat after each addition. Scrape down the inside of the bowl. Add the sesame seed meal. Blend together the remaining dry ingredients. Gradually add the mixture to the batter.

When the dough leaves the side of the bowl, turn it out onto a sprinkling of flour. Knead until the dough is smooth and elastic. Place it in an oiled bowl. Turn to coat all sides with oil. Cover. Let rise until doubled in bulk.

Punch down. Turn out on a flat surface. Press out the remaining air bubbles. Divide the dough into equal portions. Form the loaves and place in sprayed baking pans. Let rise until nearly doubled in bulk. Brush the top of the loaves with a mixture of egg white and water. Sprinkle with sesame seeds. Bake. When the loaves are finished, remove them from the pan. Cool on a rack.

NOTE: One cup of the Enrichment Mix can replace one cup of whole wheat flour called for in the recipe. Sunflower seed meal can be substituted for the sesame seed meal, if desired. The oil may be omitted since the sesame seeds contains ample fat for the recipe.

SEVEN-GRAIN BREAD

Note: In order to make this bread without taking the time to measure out all the individual cereal grains, use the Seven Grain Enrichment Mix.

OVEN TIME: 35-40 minutes at 375 degrees   **YIELD:** 2 loaves

1¼ cups water	2 teaspoons flax seed
½ cup spelt or wheat flakes	2 Tablespoons Miller's bran
2 Tablespoons amaranth	2 Tablespoons oatmeal
2 Tablespoons cornmeal	1 Tablespoon gluten
2 Tablespoons oat bran	1½ teaspoons sea salt
2 cups warm water	3 Tablespoons canola oil
2 teaspoons instant dry yeast	½ cup rye flour
3 Tablespoons brown sugar	2 cups bread flour
2 Tablespoons molasses	6½-7 cups whole wheat flour

In a medium saucepan bring the water to a boil. Sprinkle in the spelt flakes, amaranth, cornmeal and oat bran. Stir. Remove from the heat. Cool until warm to the touch. In an electric mixer bowl, dissolve the yeast in warm water. Add the brown sugar. Stir the bread flour and gluten together. Add it to the yeast mixture. Beat for 2 minutes. Add the molasses. Stir and blend.

In a separate bowl, blend together the flax, bran, and salt. Stir it into the batter. Add the cooked cereal. Scrape down the inside of the bowl. Gradually add the remaining flour. When the dough begins to leave the sides of the bowl, turn it out onto a sprinkling of flour. Knead until smooth and elastic. Place in an oiled bowl. Turn to coat all sides. Cover. Let rise until doubled in bulk. Turn it out and press out the remaining air bubbles. Form the loaves. Let rise until slightly above the top of the pan. Bake. When the bread is finished, remove it from the pans. Cool on a rack.

Note: ¾ cup of the seven-grain Enrichment Mix can replace the amaranth, cornmeal, oat bran, flax seed, bran and oatmeal. Otherwise, try adding ¾ cup of oatmeal.

"Fervency in Praise of God will eliminate all past misdeeds."
Edna Lister

SNOW WHITE AND SEVEN ODD FELLOWS

Note: This recipe has been created for people who prefer snowy white bread. Several white-colored fortifiers are added to strengthen the nutritional value of the loaf.

OVEN TIME: 30 minutes at 400 degrees   **YIELD:** 2 loaves

2 cups water	3 Tablespoons cottage cheese
1 small potato	¼ cup nonfat dry milk
¼ cup millet, cooked	¼ cup soy milk powder
2 teaspoons sea salt	¼ cup Enrichment Mix
5 teaspoons instant dry yeast	6½-7 cups unbleached white flour
3 Tablespoons honey	or all-purpose flour
2 eggs	

Cook the potato in 1 cup of water. Mash it in the cooking water. Add the millet and sea salt. Remove from the heat. Cool until warm to the touch.

In a large bowl or electric mixer bowl, dissolve the yeast in remaining warm water and add the honey. Stir to dissolve. Add 2 cups of flour to the yeast mixture. Beat 2 minutes. Scrape down the inside of the bowl. Add the eggs, one at a time. Beat after each addition. Add the potato water and the cottage cheese. Blend the nonfat dry milk, soy milk powder, and Enrichment Mix into the remaining flour. Gradually add the mixture to the batter. Scrape down the inside of the bowl.

When the dough leaves the side of the bowl, turn it out in a sprinkling of flour. Knead 6-8 minutes, or until the dough is smooth and elastic. Place the dough in an oiled bowl. Turn to coat all sides. Cover and let rise until doubled in bulk.
Press out the remaining air bubbles. Divide the dough into equal portions. Form the loaves. Place in sprayed, or oiled loaf pans. Let rise until nearly doubled in bulk. Brush with a mixture of egg white whisked in water. Bake. When the loaf is finished, remove it from the pan. Cool on a rack.

Note: ³/₈ cup flour can replace the millet, soy milk powder and Pantry Enrichment Mix.

SOUR CREAM HERBED BREAD

Note: Farm families loved to glean all possible edibles when it was time to create a recipe. The ingredient list included items from the fields, the garden, the fruit cellar, the hen house and from the pantry stores. We traded with the ''McNess Man'' and the ''Watkins Man,'' trading hens for herbs.

OVEN TIME: 30-35 minutes at 375 degrees   **YIELD:** 2 large loaves

2	cups warm potato water	2	teaspoons sea salt
4	teaspoons Saf yeast	½	cup onions, diced
	or active dry yeast	½	teaspoon oregano
¼	cup honey	½	teaspoon sage
1	cup sour cream	½	teaspoon thyme
2	eggs	4½-5	cups whole wheat flour
¼	cup nonfat dry milk	4½	cups unbleached white flour

In a large bowl or electric mixer bowl, dissolve the yeast in the warm potato water. Add the honey. Let rest until foamy. Add the white flour. Beat 2 minutes. Turn off the motor. Scrape down the side of the bowl. Add the sour cream and eggs. Beat to blend. In a separate bowl, stir together the nonfat dry milk, sea salt, oregano, sage, thyme and the remaining flour.

Gradually add the mixture to the batter. Beat after each addition. When the dough begins to climb the dough hook, turn the dough out on a flat surface onto a sprinkling of flour. Knead until smooth and elastic. Place the dough in an oiled bowl. Turn to coat all sides. Cover and let rise until doubled in bulk.

Punch the dough down. (If time allows, let the dough rise once more.) Turn it out on a flat surface and press out air bubbles. Divide the dough. Form the loaves. Place in oiled pans. Cover and let rise until nearly doubled in bulk. Brush the tops with a mixture of egg white and water. Sprinkle with oatmeal, sesame seeds, or poppy seeds. Slits may be cut in the top if desired and filled with a teaspoon of melted butter. Bake. When the loaves are finished, remove them from the pans. Cool on a rack.

NOTE: ½ cup Enrichment Mix can be substituted for ½ cup of the white flour or the whole wheat flour.

SOUTH-OF-THE-BORDER-BREAD

Note: Every one likes to have a garden party for special friends. It can be a picnic, or just a behind-the-house gathering. That's the way it was in the country where the gathering was "just out in the yard." Even the lush green side-hill by the barn was a cool place for a picnic in the days gone by. So *improvise!* Put together a mariachi washboard band, thimble castanets, washtub bongos, and a flashy table cloth. It's almost like being in Mexico.

OVEN TIME: 35-40 minutes at 375 degrees   **YIELD:** 2 large loaves
1 Mexican Pizza

2 cups warm water	1 cup buttermilk
5 teaspoons instant dry yeast	2 teaspoons sea salt
3 Tablespoons honey	2 Tablespoons gluten
⅔ cup chili, without meat	2 Tablespoons blended oil
3 Tablespoons soy milk powder	4 cups unbleached white flour
crushed tortilla chips	4½-5 cups whole wheat pastry flour
	1 cup whole kernel corn, drained

In a large mixing bowl or electric mixer bowl, dissolve the yeast in the warm water. Add the honey. If time permits, let it rest for 10 minutes. Meanwhile, open the chili con carne and the corn, drain the corn and set aside. Add 3 cups white flour to the yeast mixture. Beat 2 minutes. Scrape down the inside of the bowl. Stir the soy milk into the buttermilk; add it to the batter. Blend. Add the oil and ⅔ cup chili con carne. Blend.

In a separate bowl, stir together the remaining flour, sea salt, and gluten. Gradually add it to the batter. Beat after each addition. Scrape down the inside of the bowl. When the dough begins to leave the side of the bowl, turn it out in a sprinkling of flour.

Knead 6-8 minutes or until the dough is smooth and elastic. Place it in an oiled bowl, turn to coat all sides of the dough with oil. Cover. Let rise until doubled in bulk. Turn the dough out and press out the remaining air bubbles. Knead lightly.

Divide the dough into two 1½ lb pieces for bread, or 1 12-14 inch pizza. Roll the 2 large portions into a 10 X 14 inch rectangle. Spread with a thin layer of chili; sprinkle the drained whole kernel corn over the dough to within 1 inch on all sides. Roll the dough into a long loaf. Pinch the ends. Place the loaves seam side down into baguettes, or free-form on a baking sheet. Let rise until doubled in bulk. Brush tips lightly with 1 egg white whisked into 2 Tablespoons of water. Sprinkle with crushed tortilla chips. Bake.
Cool on a rack.

SPICY BATTER BREAD

OVEN TIME: 30 minutes at 375 degrees   **YIELD:** 1 large loaf

2 teaspoons Saf yeast	1¼ cups whole wheat
½ cup warm water	pastry flour
¼ cup brown sugar	½ cup walnuts, chopped
1 cup milk	3 cups high-protein flour
2 Tablespoons oil	¼ teaspoon ginger
3 Tablespoons dried	1 teaspoon cinnamon
fruit, chopped	½ teaspoon sea salt

Dissolve the yeast in warm water and add 1 teaspoon brown sugar. Let rest until foamy. Stir in the milk and oil. Add 2 cups high-protein flour. Beat 2 minutes. Add the dried fruit and walnuts; stir to blend. Scrape down the inside of the bowl. In a separate bowl, blend together the remaining dry ingredients. Gradually add them to the batter.

When the batter begins to leave the side of the bowl, remove the beaters. Cover and let rise in the same bowl, until nearly doubled in bulk. Stir down. Spoon into generously oiled pans. Push the batter well into the corners of the pan. Sprinkle with chopped nuts. Cover and let rise until nearly doubled in bulk. Bake. When the loaf is finished, remove it from the pans to a cooling rack.

Quick and simple method for braiding bread dough
Roll the dough to ¾ inch thick and to the desired length. With a plastic pizza cutter, cut three 1½ inch strips to within 1 inch of one end. Cross the left outside end over the middle strand, then cross the right hand strip over the middle. Repeat to the end. Pinch to seal. Glaze if desired.

> *"Nothing is ever lost, unless one declares it so."*
> *Edna Lister*

SUNFLOWER SEED BREAD

Note: The sunflower is native to the Great Plains States of the United States. The plant is valuable from both an economic and ornamental standpoint. The leaves are used for animal fodder and the flower petals for yellow dye. The oily seed provides fat, fiber, vitamins and minerals. Its protein content is in the same class as oats, wheat, barley and rye.

OVEN TIME: 35-40 minutes at 375 degrees   **YIELD:** 1 large loaf

1 cup yogurt starter	2½ cups bread flour, or
1½ warm water	unbleached white flour
1 Tablespoon instant yeast	1 Tablespoon gluten
¼ cup molasses or sorghum	1 cup rye flour
1 teaspoon sea salt	1 cup whole wheat flour
½ cup sunflower seed meal	1 egg white
2 Tablespoons sunflower oil	2 teaspoons cornmeal

In a large bowl, dissolve yeast in the warm water. Add the starter and the molasses. Add the white flour. Beat 2 minutes. In a small bowl, blend the sea salt, sunflower seed meal and gluten. Beat into the batter. Scrape down the inside of the bowl. Add the oil. Gradually add the remaining wheat flour and rye flour. Beat for 2 minutes after each addition.

When the dough begins to leave the sides of the bowl, turn it out in a sprinkling of flour. Knead until the dough becomes smooth and elastic. Shape dough into a ball. Place in an oiled bowl, turn to coat all sides. Cover with cloth and let rise in a warm place until doubled in bulk. This dough performs better when allowed to rise twice.

Turn the dough out on a flat surface. Press out the remaining air bubbles. Form into a loaf. Place in an oiled loaf pan. Allow to rise until nearly doubled in bulk. Brush with a mixture of egg white and water. Sprinkle with cornmeal. Bake. When the loaf is finished, remove it from the pan. Cool on a rack.

"Do not argue; give individuals time to defuse themselves."
Ferne Chapman

THREE-GRAIN BRAIDED BREAD

Note: Sourdough is added to this recipe not only as a flavor enhancer and leavening agent, but as a ferment to speed the partial predigestion of the phytates in cereal grains. The millet and amaranth add extra nutrients to the bread. Since both amaranth and millet are bland, dry onion soup mix is added to create more flavor. Braided loaves like this have a certain eye appeal that dinner guests love.

OVEN TIME: 30 minutes at 375 degrees   **YIELD:** 2 loaves

1 Tablespoon instant yeast	3 Tablespoons butter or oil
2½ cups warm water	¼ cup amaranth flour
3 Tablespoons honey or sugar	2 Tablespoons dry onion soup mix
1 cup sourdough starter	
¼ cup dark molasses	3 cups whole wheat flour,
½ cup cooked millet	5-5½ cups unbleached white flour

In a large bowl or electric mixer bowl, dissolve the yeast in the warm water. Add the honey. Stir to dissolve. Add 3 cups of white flour. Beat 2 minutes. Scrape down the inside of the bowl. Add the sourdough starter. Beat until blended. Add the molasses, millet and butter. Stir to blend.

In a separate bowl, blend together the remaining flour, amaranth flour and the dry onion soup mix. Gradually add the mixture to the batter. Scrape down the inside of the bowl. When the dough leaves the side of the bowl, turn it out in a sprinkling of flour. Knead 6-8 minutes, or until the dough is smooth and elastic.

Place the dough in an oiled bowl. Turn to coat all sides. Cover and let rise once (twice if time permits) until doubled in bulk. Punch down. Turn out on a flat surface and press out the remaining air bubbles. Divide the dough in half. Form 3-12'' ropes of each half and braid. Pinch the ends to seal and tuck them under. Place the braided loaves on an oiled baking sheet. Let rise until nearly doubled. Bake on the middle oven rack. Remove from the pan. Cool on a rack.

Note: The millet and amaranth may be replaced with oatmeal or barley flakes.

 Yeast Bread

THUNDERBIRD BREAD

Bread Of The Early Americans

Note: Authentic early Navajo fry bread could have been made with some type of ferment, since the non-ferment baking age began much later. This bread can be made with either the yeast method, or it can be made using baking powder and baking soda as leavening agents.

STOVE-TOP TIME: 15-20 minutes

1 cup warm water	1 Tablespoon dry onion flakes
1 Tablespoon instant dry yeast	1 teaspoon sea salt
2 Tablespoons sugar	2 Tablespoons soy milk powder
1 Tablespoon molasses	2 Tablespoons cornmeal
½ cup cooked pinto beans, mashed	2 teaspoons taco seasoning
5-6 strips of bacon, broiled, drained, crumbled	2 Tablespoons wheat germ
	2 cups unbleached white flour
	2 cups whole wheat flour

In a large bowl or electric mixer bowl, dissolve the yeast in the warm water. Add the sugar. Stir to dissolve. While letting the yeast foam, broil the bacon and drain it well. Add 2 cups white flour to the yeast mixture. Beat 2 minutes. Scrape down the inside of the bowl.

Add the molasses, mashed pinto beans, sea salt and onion flakes. Blend. Stir in the crumbled bacon. In a separate bowl, blend together the remaining flour, soy milk powder, cornmeal, taco seasoning and wheat germ. Gradually add the mixture to the batter. Scrape down the inside of the bowl. When the dough leaves the side of the bowl, turn it out onto a sprinkling of flour. Knead 6-8 minutes, or until the dough is smooth and elastic.

Place the dough in an oiled bowl. Turn to coat all sides. Cover and let rise until doubled in bulk. If time permits, let the dough rise again. Turn it out on an oiled surface. Press out the remaining air bubbles. Pinch-off plum-size balls (or larger) from the dough. Flatten each ball with the palm of the hand, into 1½- 1¾ inches in diameter. Brown each side on a lightly oiled griddle.

NOTE: The rounds make a spectacular base for taco salads. The Navajo served the fry bread with an entree of mutton stew. Sounds great to me!

TRITICALE BREAD

OVEN TIME: 30 minutes at 400 degrees   **YIELD:** 1 large loaf

1½ cups potato water	3 Tablespoons sunflower
1 cup triticale flakes	seed oil
1½ cups warm water	¼ cup soy flour
2 teaspoons Saf yeast	¼ cup ground flax seed, or
1 Tablespoon honey	New Grains Fortifier mix
¼ cup dark molasses	2 cups bread flour
¼ teaspoon ground ginger	4-4½ cups triticale flour
2 teaspoons sea salt	½ cup sunflower seeds,
	optional

In a small saucepan, bring the water, or potato water to a boil. Stir in the triticale flakes. Remove from the heat. Cool until warm to the touch.

In an electric mixer bowl, dissolve yeast in warm water Add the honey. Add 2 cups white flour. Beat 2 minutes. Stir in the molasses, ginger, oil, sea salt and sunflower seeds. Combine the triticale flour, soy flour and ground flaxseed. Gradually add it to the batter. Beat after each addition. Scrape down the inside of the bowl.

When the dough begins to leave the sides of the bowl, turn it out onto a sprinkling of flour. Knead until smooth and elastic. Place the dough in an oiled bowl, turn to coat all sides. Cover with wax paper and a cloth. Let rise until doubled in bulk.
Press out the air bubbles. Divide the dough and form into loaves. Place the loaves in an oiled loaf pan. Let rise until nearly doubled in size. Bake. If a soft crust is desired, brush with milk, cream, or oil, then bake. When the loaf is finished, remove from the pan. Cool on a rack.

"A rule has been devised that each man work on his own Honor system."
Linda Mahalic

 Yeast Bread

WARTIME BARLEY LOAVES

Note: Wartime imposed many constraints upon our life-style here in America, both during and immediately following World War I. Wheat and several other food items were in short supply.

OVEN TIME: 35-40 minutes at 400 Degrees   **YIELD:** 2 loaves

1 cup water	2 cups milk, scalded
1 small potato, diced	2 Tablespoons instant yeast
1 small onion, diced	¼ cup barley malt or honey
½ cup barley flakes	2½ cups barley flour
3 Tablespoons cornmeal	2 teaspoons sea salt
3 Tablespoons butter	4 Tablespoons millet flour
500 miligrams vitamin C	2 cups oat flour
½ teaspoon mixed herbs, optional	2½-3 cups bread flour

Scald the milk. Set aside. Cool until warm to the touch. In a saucepan, cook the diced potato and onion in the water. When the potato is cooked, mash it in the cooking water. Stir in the barley flakes, cornmeal, butter and herbs.

In a large bowl or electric mixer bowl, dissolve the yeast in the warm milk. Add the malt, or honey. Add 3 cups of bread flour. Beat for 2 minutes. Scrape down the inside of the bowl. Add the potato onion mixture and herbs to the batter. Blend well. Stir together the barley flour and the remaining bread flour.

Gradually add the blend to the batter. Beat after each addition. Scrape down the inside of the bowl. Beat until the dough begins to leave the side of the bowl. Turn it out onto a sprinkling of flour. Knead until it becomes smooth and elastic. Place the dough in an oiled bowl. Turn to coat all sides with oil. Cover with wax paper and a cloth. Let rise until doubled in bulk.

Punch down. If time allows, let the dough rise again. Turn out on an oiled surface and press out the remaining air bubbles. Divide the dough. Form the loaves. Place them in prepared pans. Let rise until nearly doubled in bulk. Bake. When the loaves are finished, remove them from the pan. Cool on a rack.

Note: If herbs are omitted, add 1 teaspoon sea salt.

WHOLE WHEAT BREAD

Note: Better nutrition is achieved by eating many different foods. This includes adding a wide variety of ingredients to each batch of bread. The simple way to do that is to use the Bread Mixes and the Enrichment Mixes.

OVEN TIME: 30 minutes at 400 degrees   **YIELD:** 2 loaves

½ cup milk, scalded	1½ teaspoons ground sage
1 cup warm water (120°F)	½ teaspoon thyme
1 egg	¾ teaspoons sea salt
2 cups Yeast Bread Mix	3-3½ cups whole wheat flour
1½ Tablespoons oil	½ cup walnuts, chopped
¾ cup Sharp Cheddar	

Heat the milk. Remove from the heat. Cool to 120 degrees. In a large bowl or electric mixer bowl, blend the milk, water, egg and oil. Add the Bread Mix. Beat 2 minutes. Add the grated cheese. Blend together the herbs, sea salt and 2 cups of the whole wheat flour. Add it to the batter. Beat well. Gradually add the remaining flour. Beat after each addition. Scrape down the inside of the bowl.

When the dough leaves the side of the bowl, turn it out onto a sprinkling of flour. Knead until it is smooth and elastic. Place the dough in an oiled bowl, turn to coat all sides of the dough with oil. Cover with wax paper and a cloth. Let rise until doubled in bulk. Punch down. Divide the dough and let it rest for 10 minutes. Form the loaves. Place in prepared pans. Let rise to nearly doubled in bulk. Bake on the middle rack of the oven. The loaves may be brushed with milk, sweet cream, oil, or butter for a soft crust. When the loaves are finished, remove them from the pan. Cool on a rack.

Note: If Yeast Bread Mix is omitted, add 2¼ teaspoons of yeast,
1 teaspoon sea salt
and 2 cups bread flour.

> *"Everyone is free to do as he, or she pleases,*
> *so long as it pleases God."*
> Edna Lister

 Yeast Bread

WILD RICE BREAD

OVEN TIME: 35 minutes at 375 degrees   **YIELD:** 2 loaves

1 small potato, diced	2 Tablespoons instant yeast
1 cup water	2 Tablespoons honey
1¼ cups milk	3 cups bread flour,
3 Tablespoons cornmeal	or unbleached white flour
3 Tablespoons oatmeal	3 cups whole wheat flour
¼ cup butter, melted	1 cup wild rice flour
¼ cup molasses	

In a small saucepan, cook the diced potato (approximately ½ cup raw potato) in 1 cup water. When cooked, mash the potato in the cooking water. Return it to the heat; stir in the milk, cornmeal, oatmeal, butter and molasses. Let heat 1 minute. Stir in the cold milk. Let the mixture heat to warm. Remove it from the heat and turn it into a large mixing bowl. Add the yeast and honey. Stir to dissolve the yeast.

Add the bread flour. Beat 2 minutes. Scrape down the inside of the bowl. In a separate bowl, blend the whole wheat flour and the wild rice flour. Gradually add it to the batter. When the dough leaves the side of the bowl, turn it out in a sprinkling of flour. Knead the dough until it becomes smooth and elastic. This dough will be a bit tacky.

Make a ball of the dough and place in an oiled bowl. Turn to coat all sides with oil. Cover with wax paper and a cloth. Let rise until doubled in bulk. Punch down. If time allows, let the dough rise a second time. Divide the dough into equal portions. Form the loaves. Place in prepared pans. Let rise until nearly doubled in bulk. Bake. When the loaves are finished, remove them from the pan. Cool on a rack.

NOTE: Zest of one orange, or 2 Tablespoons of frozen orange concentrate can bring out a new flavor in this bread. When the concentrate is added, remove 2 Tablespoons of milk.

"There is no limitation whatsoever with God,
unless you embroider yourself in limitation."
Edna Lister

YVONNE'S WHEAT HEART BREAD

Note: Deep in the heart of wheat country, in the Central States, The Carter Family celebrated a reunion. The temptation to make bread was too much for the women in the family and we baked fresh bread every day. The dough was divided for the purpose of making sticky buns, Indian Fry Bread, loaves and dinner rolls. It served 20 family members nicely. When the reunion ended, we all "rolled" home.

OVEN TIME: 35 minutes at 375 Degrees   **YIELD:** 3-4 loaves

3 cups milk, scalded	3 Tablespoons lemon juice
½ cup butter	¼ cup wheat germ
6 Tablespoons honey	4 teaspoons sea salt
2½ Tablespoons instant yeast	¼ cup non-fat dry milk
2 Tablespoons molasses	4 cups all-purpose flour
2 cups warm water	7½-8 cups whole wheat flour

Scald the milk. Remove from the heat. Stir in the butter and 5 Tablespoons honey. Set aside. Cool until warm to the touch. In a large bowl or electric mixer bowl, dissolve the yeast in the warm milk. Add the remaining honey and the molasses. Add the white flour. Beat 2 minutes. Scrape down the inside of the bowl. Add the lemon juice.

In a separate bowl, blend the wheat germ, dry milk and sea salt with the whole wheat flour. Gradually add the mixture to the batter. Beat after each addition. Scrape down the inside of the bowl. When the dough leaves the side of the bowl, turn it out in a sprinkling of flour. Knead it until it becomes smooth and elastic. Make a ball of the dough; place it in an oiled bowl. Turn to coat all sides of the dough. Cover with wax paper and a cloth. Let rise until doubled in bulk.

Divide the dough. Form the loaves or rolls. Place the loaves in prepared pans. Cover. Let rise until nearly doubled in bulk. Bake. When the loaves are finished, remove them from the pans. Cool on a rack. Brush with butter, or fresh sweet cream.

NOTE: For a smaller batch of bread, cut each ingredient by half. The mixing method remains the same.

"What we earn is our own, be it good or less good." Edna Lister

ZUCCHINI SWISS BATTER BREAD

Note: This bread is made with Swiss cheese and Jalapeno pepper cheese. Either cheese will make a tasty loaf of bread. Batter breads have a unique, craggy, brown crust. They rise one time in the mixing bowl, and one time in the baking pan before being placed in the oven.

OVEN TIME: 35-40 minutes at 400 degrees   **YIELD:** 1 long loaf

1¼ cups warm water	1 cup zucchini, coarsley grated
2 teaspoons Saf yeast	
2 Tablespooons honey	1½ cups Swiss Cheese, or Jalapeno Pepper Cheese, grated
3 Tablespoons onion, grated	
1 teaspoon sea salt	
2 Tablespoons blended oil Cheddar Cheese strips, (optional)	2 cups all-purpose flour
	1¼ cup whole wheat flour

Grate the zucchini and mince the onion. Sprinkle with ¼ teaspoon sea salt. Set aside.

In a large bowl or electric mixer bowl, dissolve the yeast in warm water and add the honey. Beat in the 2 cups white flour. Beat 2 minutes. Scrape down the inside of the bowl. Add the remaining sea salt, oil, zucchini and onion mixture and the cheese. Gradually add the remaining flour. Scrape down the inside of the bowl. Let the bread rise in the mixing bowl until nearly doubled in bulk.

Oil or spray a 10x3½x3-inch bread pan. Spoon the batter into the pan. Push the batter well into the corners of the pan. Cheddar Cheese strips can be inserted diagonally on top of the loaf, if desired. (Make small slits in the top and insert the cheese strips.) Let rise until the batter barely arches over the top of the pan. Bake 5 minutes at 400 degrees. Reduce the heat to 375 degrees and finish baking. Remove from the pan. Cool on a rack.

WHIPPING CREAM TIPS:
Place chilled whipping cream in a bowl of ice water while whipping. OR add the white of an egg to the stubborn mass, chill, then whip. Three or four drops of lemon juice may be of assistance at this time. Add ¼ teaspoon plain gelatin for each cup of cream when whipping to prevent the whipped cream from separating.

ALMOND RUM LOGS

OVEN TIME: 35-40 minutes at 375 degrees   YIELD: 2 long rolls

1 cup milk, scalded	2 Tablespoons gluten
1 cup warm water	6½-7 cups unbleached
1 Tablespoon instant	white flour
dry yeast	FILLING:
¼ cup sugar or honey	¼ cup hot milk
2 eggs	2 Tablespoons butter
1 cup plain yogurt,	4 ounces almond paste
or sour cream	2 Tablespoons rum
¼ cup nonfat dry milk,	½ cup brown sugar
or soy milk	¼ teaspoon nutmeg

Heat the milk. Set aside. Cool until warm to the touch. In a large bowl or electric mixer bowl, dissolve the yeast in the warm water and add 1 Tablespoon sugar. Add the warm milk. Add 3 cups flour. Beat 2 minutes. Beat in the eggs, one at a time. Stir in the yogurt and remaining sugar. Blend the gluten and non-fat milk with 2 cups flour. Add the mixture to the batter. Beat 2 minutes. Scrape down the inside of the bowl. Gradually add the remaining flour. Beat after each addition. Scrape down the inside of the bowl.

When the dough begins to leave the side of the bowl, turn it out onto a sprinkling of flour. Knead until it becomes smooth and elastic. Place the dough in an oiled bowl. Turn to coat all sides. Cover and let rise until doubled in bulk.
Punch the dough down. Turn out on a flat surface. Press out the remaining air bubbles. Divide the dough and let rest for 8-10 minutes. Prepare the filling. Heat the milk. Stir in all of the filling ingredients. Cook until slightly thickened. Let the filling cool slightly.

Roll each piece of dough into a rectangle, ½ inch thick. Spread each rectangle with half of the filling. Roll each into a long roll. Pinch the end of the dough to seal. Place them on an oiled baking sheet. Brush with beaten egg white and 1 Tablespoon water. Sprinkle with slivered almonds. Let rise until nearly doubled in bulk. Bake on the middle rack of the oven. Cool on a rack. Slice to serve.

"Truth is a jewel, wear it daily."
Edna Lister

APPLE CHEESE DEEP DISH DESSERT

Note: This German Deep Dish Dessert crust is made with yeast dough. It is so filling and sweet that one slice is nearly a meal in itself.

OVEN TIME: 45-50 minutes at 375 degrees   **YIELD:** 2-Deep Dish pies

1 cup Convenience Mix	**FILLING:**
¾ cup warm water	6-8 medium apples
1 egg, separated	¾ cup sugar
1½ Tablespoons oil	½ teaspoon nutmeg
1 Tablespoon honey	⅛ teaspoon sea salt
½ cup Cheddar cheese, grated	1 teaspoon cinnamon
½ teaspoon cinnamon	2 teaspoons lemon juice
1½ cups unbleached white flour	1 cup Sharp Cheddar cheese, grated
	2 Tablespoons flour or cornstarch

Measure the Convenience Mix into a large bowl. In a small bowl, beat together the egg, water and oil. Blend all ingredients together. Knead well. Divide the dough.

Cover. Let it rest for 10 minutes. Roll the dough to the size needed, or press the dough into an oiled pan, working the dough up the sides. Flute the edges slightly. Brush the bottom of the crust with the lightly whisked egg yolk. Bake 5-6 minutes. Remove from the oven. Prepare the filling.

FILLING:
Slice the apples and chop slightly. In a small bowl, blend together the remaining ingredients. Stir it into the apples. Spoon the apples into the crusts. If a top crust is desired, roll a small portion of the dough, cut slits into the center and cover the pie. Seal the edges. Bake. If the crust browns too rapidly, cover the pie lightly with a pan.

When the apples are cooked and the crust brown, remove the dish from the oven. Cool slightly before serving.

Note: This crust will brown rapidly. The apples may be lightly steamed before putting the filling together, or you may wish to cover the pie while baking with parchment paper or foil. Remove 15 minutes before the pie is completely baked.

BARELY BARLEY SWEET TWISTS

OVEN TIME: 25 minutes at 375 Degrees   **YIELD:** 12-14 twists

2 cups milk	FILLING:
¼ cup barley flakes	⅔ cup brown sugar
2 Tablespoons butter, softened	1 Tablespoon orange peel, grated, or candied fruit
1 teaspoon sea salt	½ teaspoon cinnamon
2 teaspoons Saf yeast	FROSTING:
½ cup sugar	3 ounces cream cheese
2 eggs	2½ cups powdered sugar
¼ cup sour cream	2-3 teaspoons milk or cream
⅛ teaspoon vanilla, optional	
5½-6 cups unbleached white flour	

In a small saucepan, heat the milk to near boiling. Remove from the heat and stir in the barley flakes, butter and sea salt. Set aside. Cool until warm to the touch. In a large bowl or electric mixer bowl, dissolve the yeast in the warm milk mixture. Add 1 Tablespoon of the sugar. Add 2 cups of flour. Beat 2 minutes. Add the remaining sugar. Beat in the eggs, one at a time. Add the sour cream. Scrape down the inside of the bowl.

Gradually add the remaining flour. Beat after each addition. When the dough begins to leave the side of the bowl, turn it out onto a sprinkling of flour. Knead lightly. Form a ball of the dough and place it in an oiled bowl. Turn to coat all sides of the dough with oil. Cover and let rise until doubled in bulk. While the dough rises, mix the filling. Set aside.

Knead the dough down. Divide it in half. Roll each half into a rectangle, 9 x 14 inches. Spread the rectangle with butter or sour cream. Sprinkle half of the filling over half of the rectangle. Gently fold the other half over the top of the filling. Bring the folded side toward you. Flatten and straighten the dough layer. Using a ruler and a plastic pizza cutter or a sharp knife, cut ⅓ inch strips away from the fold, through both layers. Grip the ends of each strip and twist in opposite directions, until the strip resembles a rope. Twist the rope into a figure 8. Place it on an oiled baking sheet. Pinch the ends of the rope to hold the shape. For entertaining guests, a variety of shapes arranged nicely on a decorative plate will add interest to the setting. When the twists are cooled, mix the frosting and spread as desired over the swirls. Slivered almonds may be sprinkled over the frosting.

JULEBROD—NORWEGIAN CHRISTMAS BREAD

One of our Norweigian neighbors taught my mother how to prepare Norwegian dishes from our simple farm fare. This bread was one of the few sweet treats we enjoyed during the Christmas season.

OVEN TIME: 35 minutes at 375 Degrees   **YIELD:** 2 loaves

1¼ cup milk, scalded	1 teaspoon sea salt
¼ cup butter	¼ teaspoon ground ginger
¼ cup oatmeal	1 teaspoon ground cardamom
¼ cup honey	3 Tablespoons rum
½ cup warm water	3 Tablespoons orange zest
4 teaspoons dry yeast	½ cup blanched almonds, chopped
1 teaspoon sugar	¼ cup golden raisins or currants
2 eggs	5½-6 cups all-purpose flour

Heat the milk in a medium saucepan. Stir in the butter, oatmeal, and honey. Remove from the heat. Allow the mixture to cool to room temperature. Dissolve the yeast in the warm water and add the sugar. In a large bowl or electric mixer bowl, combine the oatmeal and the yeast mixtures. Add 2 cups flour. Beat 2 minutes. Scrape down the inside of the bowl. Add the eggs, one at a time. Beat after each egg.

In a small bowl, combine the remaining dry ingredients. Stir the rum, orange zest, nuts and raisins into the egg mixture. Gradually add the dry ingredients to the batter. When the dough leaves the side of the bowl, turn it out onto a sprinkling of flour. Knead until it is smooth and elastic. Sprinkle flour over the dough only as needed. This is a soft and pliable dough. Place the dough in an oiled bowl. Turn to coat all sides. Cover and let rise until doubled in bulk. Punch down. Turn out on a flat surface. Press out the remaining air bubbles.

Divide the dough in half. Cut each half into 3 equal pieces. Using your palms, roll the dough into ropes, approximately 30-inches long. Place the ropes parallel to each other. Beginning in the middle, braid the ropes to each end. Pinch the ends together to secure them. Place the braided loaves on an oiled baking sheet. Let rise to nearly doubled in bulk. Bake. When the loaves are finished, remove from the pan. Cool on a rack.

PEACHES AND CREAM CINNAMON ROLLS

This batch of rolls is sweetened with tidbits of home-canned peaches in the juice that might otherwise be thrown away. The texture and unique peachy-almond flavor may inspire someone to preserve peaches next harvest time.

OVEN TIME: 35-40 minutes at 375 degrees   **YIELD:** 16-18 rolls

1 cup peach liquid	3 Tablespoons instant dry milk
2 peach halves	1 Tablespoon gluten
1 Tablespoon instant dry yeast	2 Tablespoons Enrichment Mix, optional
2 Tablespoons sugar	1 teaspoon almond flavoring
1 cup sweet cream, warm	1 teaspoon sea salt
¼ cup butter	⅔ cup slivered almonds
2 eggs	5½-6 cups all-purpose flour

Puree the peach halves in the peach liquid. Heat until warm. Set aside. In a large bowl or electric mixer bowl, dissolve the yeast in the warm liquid. Add the sugar. Stir to dissolve. Add the warm cream, butter, eggs and almond flavoring. Add 2 cups flour. Beat 2 minutes.

In a separate small bowl, mix the dry milk, gluten, Enrichment Mix and remaining sea salt. Gradually add it to the batter. Scrape down the inside of the bowl. When the dough begins to leave the side of the bowl, turn it out onto a sprinkling of flour. Knead well. Place the dough in an oiled bowl. Turn to coat all sides. Cover. Let rise until doubled in bulk.
Punch the dough down. Turn it out on a flat surface. Press out the remaining air bubbles. Generously grease the baking pan with butter. Sprinkle a fine layer of brown sugar, chopped nuts, raisins and cinnamon over the butter. Set aside. Roll the dough into a rectangle approximately 12 x 24 inches. Spread with softened butter or sour cream. Sprinkle with a mixture of cinnamon and sugar.

Roll the dough across the full width. Pinch the end to secure. Place the dough seam-side down. Slice the roll 1-1½ inches thick. Place the cut-end down in the prepared pan. Place the rolls ¼ inch apart. This gives them room to rise. Cover. Let rise until doubled. Bake on the middle rack of the oven. Set the cooling rack on a baking sheet before inverting the hot rolls.

POPPY SEED ROLL

OVEN TIME: 30-35 minutes at 350 degrees   **YIELD:** 1 loaf

3½ cups high-gluten flour
2 teaspoons Saf yeast
1 cup hot water
3 Tablespoons soy milk
   powder, or nonfat dry milk
2 Tablespoons butter, melted
2 Tablespoons sour cream

¼ cup sugar
2 Tablespoons frozen
   lemonade concentrate
1 teaspoon sea salt
1 egg
1 cup poppy seeds, ground
   or finely chopped walnuts
¾ cup sugar
½ cup milk
1 Tablespoon lemon zest

In an electric mixer bowl, stir together 2 cups flour, 1 teaspoon sugar and the yeast. Add 1 cup hot water (120-130 degrees) and begin beating immediately. Beat 2 minutes. If time allows, let the mixture rest for 10 minutes.

Stir the soy milk powder into the remaining flour, sugar and salt. Set aside. Beat in the lemonade concentrate, butter and sour cream. Beat 2 minutes. Scrape down the inside of the bowl. Gradually add the remaining flour. When the dough leaves the side of the bowl, turn it out onto a sprinkling of flour. Knead until the dough is smooth and elastic. Place it in an oiled bowl. Turn to coat all sides. Cover and let rise until doubled in bulk. Punch down. In a separate small saucepan, or doubled-boiler, add the beaten egg, sugar, milk, lemon zest and poppy seeds. Cook over low heat for 10 minutes, stirring constantly. Remove from heat, set aside.

Turn the dough out on a flat surface. Press out the remaining air bubbles. Roll into a rectangle of approximately 10x17-inches. Spread the dough with the poppy seed mixture. Roll like a jelly roll. Pinch the ends together to secure them. With a long spatula, lift the roll onto an oiled baking sheet, seam side down. (The roll may be cut in half and baked in a loaf pan, or sliced and baked cinnamon roll-style.)

Cover and let rise until nearly doubled in bulk. Brush the loaf with a mixture of 1 egg white and 2 Tablespoons water, whisked together. For a dark, shiny crust brush with 1 egg yolk, whisked in 1½ Tablespoons water. Bake. When the loaf is finished, remove it from the pan. Cool on a rack.

RUSSIAN CEREMONIAL BREAD

OVEN TIME: 35-40 minutes at 350 Degrees   **YIELD:** 1 tall loaf

¼ cup mashed potatoes	1¼ teaspoons almond flavoring
1 cup warm water	¼ cup butter, melted
1 Tablespoon instant dry yeast	4 eggs, separated
⅔ cup sugar	½ cup slivered almonds, or sunflower seeds
¾ cup heavy cream	7-7½ cups unbleached white flour

Cook one small potato in the water. Mash the potato in the cooking water. Cool until warm to the touch. Add the warm water, yeast and 1 teaspoon sugar. Stir to dissolve. Add the heavy cream. Add 2 cups flour. Beat 2 minutes. Scrape down the inside of the bowl. Add all but 2 teaspoons of the remaining sugar, flavoring and melted butter. Beat in the egg yolks, one at a time. Add 2½-3 cups flour. Beat well.

In a separate bowl, beat the egg whites with the remaining 2 teaspoons of sugar until stiff but moist. Stir approximately 1 cup of the bread batter into the beaten whites. Fold the whites back into the dough. Carefully work the remainder of the flour into the dough. This is a very smooth and pliable dough.

Place the dough in an oiled bowl; turn to coat all sides. Cover and let rise until doubled in bulk. Turn out onto a sprinkling of flour. Press out the remaining air bubbles. Mold the loaf and place in a tall, generously greased can, kettle or other container. Let rise until nearly doubled, or until it is 1/2-inch above the top of the container. Move the oven rack down to accommodate the larger loaf. Bake.

NOTE: Drizzle the top of the loaf with Confectioners sugar frosting. Let the frosting spill down the sides of the loaf. Sprinkle with slivered almonds, candied fruit or crushed candy canes.

"Make Praise a gray-day practice, it will attract The Son!"
Edna Lister

82   **Sweet Breads**

RUSTIC STOLLEN

OVEN TIME: 30-35 minutes at 375 Degrees   **YIELD:** 2 loaves

1 cup dried currants, or raisins	5-5½ cups unbleached white flour
2 cups whole milk	⅔ cup walnuts, chopped
5 teaspoons dry yeast	FILLING:
½ cup sugar	½ cup cottage cheese, pureed
¼ cup butter, melted	½ teaspoon cinnamon
2 teaspoons vanilla flavoring	¼ cup sour cream
¼ cup sour cream	¼ cup sugar
2 eggs	1 egg yolk
3 cups whole wheat flour	1 egg white, for topping

Rinse the raisins or currants in warm water. Drain. Set aside. Heat the milk. Cool until warm to the touch. Turn the milk into a large bowl, dissolve the yeast and add 2 Tablespoons sugar. Let rest until foamy. Add 3 cups flour. Beat 2 minutes. Add the remaining sugar and the butter, vanilla, sour cream and eggs. Beat well. Add the raisins or currants. Scrape down the inside of the bowl. Stir in the walnuts. Gradually add the remaining flour. When the dough leaves the side of the bowl, turn it out on a flat surface. Knead until the dough becomes smooth and elastic. Add sprinkles of flour if needed to prevent stickiness.

Place the dough in an oiled bowl. Turn to coat all sides. Cover and let rise until doubled in bulk. Punch down and turn out on a flat surface. Press out the remaining air bubbles. Divide the dough in half. Roll each piece into a rectangle, approximately 10 inches x 7-8 inches. Prepare the filling, divide and spread over half of the rectangle. Fold lengthwise, almost in half, leaving 1¼ inch of the flap uncovered. Place on an oiled baking sheet. Repeat the procedure for the second loaf. Place on an oiled baking sheet. Let rise until doubled in bulk. Brush with a mixture of 1 egg white and 1 Tablespoon of water. Bake 5-8 minutes. Brush again with egg white mixture. Halfway into the baking cycle, turn the stollen around in the oven for even browning. Remove from the oven, brush with melted butter. Sift powdered sugar over the loaves.

To prepare the filling, beat the egg yolk and cheese together. Blend in the remaining ingredients. Spread inside the lower flap of the stollen. Seal the edges by pinching, or by pressing with tines of a fork.

SCHNECKEN

OVEN TIME: 35-40 minutes at 375 Degrees   **YIELD:** 12 Large Rolls

½ cup warm milk	1 teaspoon sea salt
1 cup warm water	1 cup sour cream
1 Tablespoon instant dry yeast	500 milligrams vitamin C, crushed
½ cup sugar	7½-8 cups all-purpose flour
¼ cup butter, melted	½ cup walnuts, chopped, (optional)
2 eggs	¾ cup raisins
2 Tablespoons soy milk powder	½-1 teaspoon cinnamon

Heat the milk. Set aside. Cool until warm to the touch. In a large bowl or electric mixer bowl, dissolve the yeast in the warm water and add 1 teaspoon sugar. Let rest until the mixture becomes foamy. Add the milk and the remaining sugar. Blend. Add 4 cups flour. Beat 2 minutes. Add the melted butter. Stir to blend. Add the eggs, one at a time. Beat after each addition. Scrape down the inside of the bowl.

Stir in the sour cream. Blend the sea salt and soy milk powder with the remaining flour, vitamin C and gradually add it to the batter. Beat after each addition. Scrape down the inside of the bowl. When the dough leaves the sides of the bowl, turn it out onto a sprinkling of flour. Knead lightly. Place the dough in an oiled bowl. Turn to coat all sides with oil. Cover. Let rise until doubled in bulk. Turn out on a flat surface and press out the remaining air bubbles. Divide the dough in half. Roll each into a rectangle to ½ inch thick.

Spread the top with softened butter. Sprinkle with cinnamon and sugar. Add the raisins. Roll across the width like a jelly roll. Seal the edges by pinching them together. Cut 1½ inch slices. Spoon the sweet glaze into the well buttered pan. Place the cut-side down in the sweet glaze. Cover. Allow to rise in a warm place until doubled in bulk. Bake. Place a baking sheet under the cooling rack. When the rolls are finished, invert the pan immediately on the cooling rack. (Grip the pan with hotpads and invert.) The glaze will drip into the pan below. Frost if desired.

> *"One must balance giving with receiving.*
> *So get on the giving end of compassion."*
> *Edna Lister*

 Sweet Breads

General instructions for bread machines:
Place all ingredients into the baking pan in the order listed, or add the yeast after the flour. Insert the baking pan securely into the bread machine. Select the desired baking cycle.

When the cycle is complete, remove the baking pan using hotpads. Remove the bread from the pan. Cool on a rack.

When using the Dough Setting, the machine will sound a tone or flash a light to indicate that the first rising is finishing. Remove the dough from the pan. Knead in a sprinkle of flour for one minute. Form the loaf and place it in an oiled pan. Cover and let rise until nearly doubled in bulk. Bake.

Bake large loaves for 30 minutes at 400 degrees. Bake smaller loaves (4 X 7 X 3) for 25-30 minutes at 400 degrees.

Ideas to cut down baking time:
You can make several batches of bread by taking advantage of the Dough Setting. Prepare the ingredients as usual, but after the first rising remove the dough from the bread machine. Form the loaf and slip into a plastic bag, pressing out excess air. Seal the plastic bag and place inside a heavy paper bag. Freeze. (The heavy paper will help prevent freezer burn if you don't use the loaf within 2-3 weeks.)

Before baking, thaw the loaf for 30-60 minutes. Bake as usual.

What went wrong with the loaf?
Using bread machines in high altitudes sometimes results in poorly raised loaves. Try grinding the flour very fine and reducing the yeast by $\frac{1}{4}$-$\frac{1}{8}$ teaspoon until the loaves rise higher. Freshly ground cereal grains will work better than flour that has been sitting on the shelf for an extended period of time. Flour that is still warm from the grinder seems especially effective in producing a quality loaf.
If the sides of the loaf cave in, then too much liquid is present. Reduce any added liquid in the recipe in 1-2 teaspoon increments until the loaf firms up. (Humid weather will make the flour more absorbent. *(Con't)*

The reverse is true during hot, dry weather: add an additional 1-2
teaspoons of liquid.)

When introducing non-wheat or non-glutenous grains to a recipe, add them
in small amounts at first. Increase the amount of the new grain by 1-2
Tablespoons until you find a ratio that works for you.

All of the yeast bread recipes in this book can be made using the Dough
or Menu setting on the bread machine. However, always check the instruc-
tion book for your machine to determine the best ratio of liquid to dry
ingredients.

Loaves that do not rise may contain too much flour, insufficient yeast, old
flour, or too much non-gluten flour. Adding vitamin C (¼-½ teaspoon) or
gluten (1-2 Tablespoon) might help. (Some of the enrichment mixes
already contain vitamin C.)

Ideas for bread machines:
Since the bread machines are primarily designed for wheat flour, you may
have to experiment when adding grains, grasses, or herbs to the bread.
Bromated bread flour is recommended for most machines; however, high-
gluten flour can also be used with success. Potassium Bromate is added
to the flour to strengthen the gluten strands against the stress of
mechanical dough beaters.

Make your own high gluten flour
Add 3 Tablespoons gluten (not gluten flour) to each 3-5 cups of unbleached white flour, or all-purpose flour in the recipe. vitamin C powder, whey
powder, barley malt, dry vinegar and soy flour, or soy milk powder can
boost the rising power and nutritional content of the loaf.

When the recipe calls for fresh or dried fruits, consider reducing the
amount of added sugar in the recipe. Drain and blot the fruit with a paper
towel before adding.

Consider reducing any added fat when the recipe calls for sour cream,
sweet cream or whole milk.

SPECIAL NEW ADDITION FOR BREAD MACHINES

Due to the increased popularity of bread machine baking and the limited amount of nutrients that are generally incorporated into each loaf, I would advise everyone to create your own nutritionally dense recipes. The new creations will recapture the "old world" quality, texture, and flavor . Bread enthusiasts everywhere are welcoming new innovative creations which fit individual cultures and contain flavors which compliment the dishes being served.

Breads made with inferior flour and diminished nutrients may make a fine appearing loaf of bread, however, many are a disappointment to the palate. Flour blends and fortifiers which appear at the beginning of this book will replace all nutrients which have been removed from the flour during the milling process. Simply select 3-8 ingredients from the listings, blend them together and add 2 Tablespoons of the flour blends to each loaf of bread. It will be necessary to remove 2 Tablespoons of flour called for in the recipe.

NOTE: ALL RECIPES ARE BAKED USING THE WHITE BREAD SETTING, UNLESS SPECIFIED. ALL RECIPES ARE FOR 1½ POUND LOAF SIZE.

TROUBLE SHOOTING TIPS:

- All bread recipes can be converted for use in the bread machine, no matter which size machine one uses.

- Recipes that call for approximately 6 cups of flour work well without to much effort for the baker. Simply divide the ingredients by 2 for the 1½ pound bread machine and divide by 3 for the 1 pound machine. The yeast, however, is a different story. It will take 2 teaspoons of fast-rising yeast for the large loaf and 1½ for the small loaf.

- When whole grains, non-gluten grains, and dried fruits or other heavier ingredients are added, the success of the loaf then depends upon a Tablespoon or two of gluten or a bit more yeast.

- Begin the increase of yeast by only ⅛ teaspoon per each large loaf of "hearty" grains. If the bread is too dense, a teaspoon of lemon juice or crushed 200mg of ascorbic acid tablet or ½ teaspoon more of yeast may be added next time.

Bread Machine 1

- Because <u>ALL BREAD FLOUR IS NOT EQUAL IN PROTEIN VALUE,</u> it is well to add extra wheat gluten.

- 12% gluten will yield a medium rising loaf. By adding 1-2 Tablespoons of wheat gluten to the large loaf, the rising power can be greatly increased.

- It is good to keep a close check on the dough during the first mixing cycle, sometimes only a teaspoon or two of either flour or water may be needed to form the proper consistency of dough. If the dough is smearing in the bottom of the pan, add 1 teaspoon flour until the dough spins freely.

- The dough must form a soft well formed ball that will spin around in the pan easily, without smearing in the bottom of the container.

- If the ball of dough takes on a firm and cylindrical form, add 1 teaspoon liquid at a time until the dough forms a softer ball which leaves the sides of the baking pan easily.

- For the sake of food safety, it is good to scrub the inside of the baking pan with a mild solution of household bleach water and/or hot soapy water using a soft bristle brush. Rinse well. (household bleach water consists of 1 Tablespoon of bleach to 1 gallon of water).

- Salt and sugar ratios are extremely important to successful bread making. Sugar is needed to make the yeast rise. Salt is needed not only for flavor, but it will inhibit over-rising as well.

- Non-gluten grain and legume additions should not exceed 1 Tablespoon per cup of flour used, unless extra gluten is added to the loaf.

Bread Machine

APPLE ALMOND MULTI-FLAKE BREAD

1	cup + 1 Tablespoon water	½	cup diced apple
¼	cup apple concentrate	3	Tablespoons gluten
2	teaspoons honey	⅓	cup mixed flakes
2	Tablespoons lemon juice	2¼	cups bread flour
2	teaspoons lemon zest	¾	cup whole wheat flour
1	teaspoon salt	¼	cup slivered almonds
2	Tablespoons oil	2¼	teaspoons Saf yeast

Place all ingredients into the baking pan. Bake. Cool on a rack.

BASIC NEW GRAINS BROWN BREAD WITH SUN DRIED TOMATOES

1	cup + 2 Tablespoons milk	⅛	teaspoon garlic powder
2	Tablespoons lemon juice	1	teaspoon salt
2	Tablespoons sugar	1	cup kamut flour
2	Tablespoons oil	1	cup spelt flour
3	Tablespoons gluten	1	cup bread flour
3	Tablespoons diced sun dried tomatoes	2	teaspoons Saf yeast

Place the ingredients into the baking pan. Bake using the rye bread cycle on your machine. Press memory button on the second rise. Let the dough rise 45 minutes to 1 hour. (until it reaches near the top of the pan). Press bake. Cool on a rack.

BRAZIL NUT PRUNE BRAN BREAD

½	cup prune juice	2	Tablespoons wheat germ
⅔	cup water	2	Tablespoons wheat bran
1	Tablespoon honey	2½	cups bread flour
¾	teaspoon salt	½	cup whole wheat flour
1½	Tablespoons oil	2	teaspoons Saf yeast
1	Tablespoon gluten	⅓	cup chopped brazil nuts
1	Tablespoon lemon juice	⅓	cup cooked, cut prunes

Place the ingredients into the baking pan. Bake. Cool on a rack.

BROWN RICE WHEAT WALNUT BREAD

1¼	cups water	3	Tablespoons gluten
2	Tablespoons dry buttermilk	⅓	cup brown rice flour
2	Tablespoons maple syrup or honey	1¼	cups bread flour
1½	Tablespoons oil	1½	cups whole wheat flour
4	teaspoons lemon juice	2	teaspoons Saf yeast
1	teaspoon salt	½	cup chopped walnuts

Place the ingredients into the baking pan. Bake. Cool on a rack.

BUTTERMILK SQUASH APRICOT CASHEW BREAD

Cook 1½ cups squash with 15 diced dried apricots. Cool and puree.

¾	cup water + 2 Tablespoons	1	teaspoon cinnamon
½	cup squash/apricot puree	2	Tablespoons gluten
2	Tablespoons maple syrup	1	Tablespoon buttermilk powder
1½	Tablespoons oil	½	cup whole wheat flour
1	Tablespoon lemon juice	2½	cups bread flour
1	teaspoon salt	2	teaspoons Saf yeast
		¼	cup chopped cashew nuts

Place all the ingredients into the baking pan in the order listed. Bake. Cool on a rack.

BUTTERMILK SUNFLOWER CILANTRO

½	cup buttermilk	2½	cups bread flour
⅓	cup water	2	Tablespoons Kamut/Quinoa (see page 9)
2	Tablespoons lemon juice		
2	Tablespoons oil	3	Tablespoons sunflower seeds
2	Tablespoons honey	½	cup grated swiss,or romano cheese
1	teaspoon salt		
3	Tablespoons gluten	2	Tablespoons ground flax seeds
2	Tablespoons chopped cilantro	2⅛	teaspoons fast-rising yeast

Place the ingredients into the baking pan. Bake. Cool on a rack. This bread has a cake-like texture due to the added mix.

CALIFORNIA SOURDOUGH DILL CHEESE BREAD

1	cup water	3	cups bread flour
2	Tablespoons powdered buttermilk	2	Tablespoons California Sour-do Powder
1	medium egg		
1	Tablespoon sugar	1	Tablespoon gluten
1	teaspoon salt	1	Tablespoon non-fat dry milk
2	Tablespoons oil	¼	cup grated Parmesan cheese
1	Tablespoon dill weed	2	teaspoons Saf yeast

Place the ingredients into the baking pan. Bake. Cool on a rack.

CHOCOLATE ZUCCHINI BREAD

1	cup milk	3	Tablespoons cocoa
2	Tablespoons brown sugar	1	Tablespoon gluten
1	egg	2½	cups bread flour plus 1 Tablespoon
1	teaspoon salt		
2	Tablespoons oil	⅓	cup whole wheat flour
1	teaspoon lemon juice	2	Tablespoons wheat germ
¼	cup grated, drained zucchini	¼	cup chopped walnuts
		2	teaspoons Saf Yeast

Place all ingredients into the baking pan. Bake. Cool on a rack.

Note: Gluten is added to most of the recipes because, not all bread flour has a high enough gluten content to make a high rising loaf of bread.

DRIED OLIVE SAGE ASIAGO CHEESE BREAD

1¼	cups warm water	2	Tablespoons Kamut/Quinoa (see page 9)
1	Tablespoon sugar		
1	teaspoon salt	2⅓	cups bread flour
1½	Tablespoons oil	¼	cup whole wheat flour
2	Tablespoons Sour-do powder	2	Tablespoons gluten
1	Tablespoon lemon juice	2	teaspoons fast-rising yeast
1	teaspoon ground sage	¼	cup diced dried olives
		¼	cup Asiago cheese, shredded

Place all ingredients into the baking pan. Bake. Cool on a rack.

FIVE-GRAIN WARTIME BREAD

1½	cups water		2	Tablespoons wheat germ
2	Tablespoons buttermilk-powder		¼	cup gluten
2	Tablespoons honey or maple sugar		½	cup mixed oat, barley, rye spelt flour
1½	Tablespoons oil		2½	cups bread flour
1	teaspoon salt		½	cup diced chedder cheese
1	Tablespoon lemon juice		2	teaspoons Saf Yeast

Place the ingredients into the baking pan. Bake. Cool on a rack.

FANTASTIC FLAKES BREAD

1¼	cups water		2	Tablespoons wheat germ
1	egg		⅓	cup whole wheat flour
2	Tablespoons butter		2½	cups bread flour
2½	Tablespoons sugar		1	cup robust & hearty flake mix,(1st 5 ingredients, page 12)
1	teaspoon salt			
2	teaspoon lemon juice		2	teaspoons Saf Yeast
2	Tablespoons gluten			

Place all the ingredients into the baking pan in the order listed. Bake. Cool on a rack.

FAMILY FAVORITE BREAD

1	cup buttermilk or sour milk		1	Tablespoons cornmeal
1	medium egg		¼	cup mixed flakes
1	Tablespoon honey		2	teaspoons pizza seasoning
1	Tablespoon molasses		2	Tablespoons gluten
1½	Tablespoon oil		1¼	cups whole wheat flour
1	teaspoon salt		1½	cups bread flour
2	teaspoons lemon juice		2	teaspoons Saf Yeast

Place all the ingredients into the baking pan in the order listed. Bake. Cool on a rack.

FATHER'S "OLD WORLD" BREAD

1¼	cups apple juice		⅓	cup whole wheat flour
2	Tablespoons oil		2	Tablespoons oat bran
1½	Tablespoons brown sugar		½	cup Miller's bran
1	teaspoon salt		¼	cup grated carrots
¼	cup cooked winter squash		¼	cup snipped prunes
1	Tablespoon gluten		4	dried apricots, diced
2⅞	cups bread flour		2	teaspoons Saf Yeast

Place all the ingredients into the baking pan in the order listed. Bake. Cool on a rack.

FERMENTED WHEAT BERRY BREAD

Soak ¼ cup whole wheat berries in 1 cup of the same water for three days. Strain. Reserve the berries and water. Lightly chop the wheat berries.

1¼	cups wheat water		3	Tablespoons gluten
2	Tablespoons molasses		¼	cup wheat berries
1	teaspoon sugar		2½	cups bread flour
1	teaspoon salt		½	cup whole wheat flour
1½	Tablespoons oil		2⅛	teaspoons Saf Yeast

Place all the ingredients into the baking pan in the order listed. Bake. Cool on a rack.

FLAX SEED, MILLET, SUN-DRIED TOMATO BREAD

1¼	cups water		2	Tablespoons flax seed
2	Tablespoons honey or maple syrup		2¾	cups bread flour
3	Tablespoons dry buttermilk		½	cup whole wheat flour
1	teaspoon salt		1	Tablespoon gluten
1½	Tablespoons oil		3	Tablespoons whole millet
¼	cup millet flour		2	teaspoons Saf yeast
			⅓	cup Sun-Dried tomatoes

Place all the ingredients into the baking pan in the order listed. Bake. Cool on a rack.

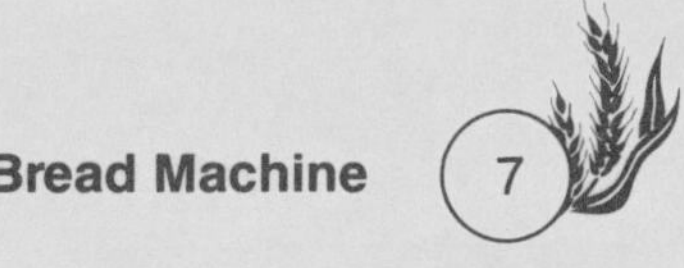

GREEK HERB BUTTERMILK BREAD

1 cup buttermilk	1/3 cup cornmeal
1/4 cup water	2 Tablespoons gluten
2 Tablespoons oil	2 Tablespoons wheat germ
2 Tablespoons honey	1/2 cup whole wheat flour
1/8 teaspoon white pepper	2 cups bread flour
1 teaspoon salt	2 teaspoons Saf yeast
	2 teaspoons Greek herb blend

Place all the ingredients into the baking pan in the order listed. Bake. Cool on a rack. (herbs: oregano, marjoram, basil, mint, rosemary, cumin, and garlic.)

GRUYERE CHEESE GARLIC BREAD

1 1/4 cups water	2 Tablespoons gluten
2 Tablespoons sugar	1/3 cup mixed cereal flakes: rye
3 Tablespoons dry buttermilk powder	wheat, barley, and spelt
1/2 teaspoon salt	2 1/2 cups bread flour
1/4 teaspoon garlic flakes	2 teaspoons Saf yeast
2 Tablespoons oil	1/2 cup grated Gruyere cheese

Place all the ingredients into the baking pan in the order listed. Bake. Cool on a rack.

KASSARI CHEESE FOUR-GRAIN BREAD

1 1/4 cups water or apple juice	1/4 cup gluten
2 Tablespoons dry buttermilk powder	1/4 cup spelt or barley flour
2 Tablespoons honey	2 1/2 cups bread flour
1 teaspoons salt	2 teaspoons Saf yeast
1 Tablespoon oil	1/3 cup grated Kassari cheese

Place all the ingredients into the baking pan in the order listed. Bake. Cool on a rack. Whole wheat flour may replace spelt/barley.

KAMUT QUINOA CANDIED ORANGE PEEL BREAD

1	cup water	½	cup chopped dried cranberries
¼	cup plain yogurt	1¾	cups bread flour
2	Tablespoons butter	1¼	cups Kamut/Quinoa Mix
¾	teaspoon salt	3	Tablespoons candied orange peel
2	Tablespoons honey		
3	Tablespoons gluten	2	teaspoons Saf yeast
½	teaspoon cinnamon		

Place all the ingredients into the baking pan in the order listed. Bake. Cool on a rack.
Mix: 2 cups kamut flour, 1 cup quinoa, 2 cups brown rice flour, 1 cup millet flour, ½ cup buckwheat flour, ¼ cup red or yellow lentil flour, ½ cup ground flax seed.

LEMON POPPY SEED BREAD

1¼	cups water	2	Tablespoons dry buttermilk powder
2	Tablespoons maple syrup		
1	teaspoon salt	1½	teaspoons poppy seeds
1	Tablespoon lemon juice	1	Tablespoon wheat germ
2	teaspoons lemon zest	1	Tablespoon gluten
1½	Tablespoons oil	2	cups bread flour + 2 teaspoons
		2	teaspoons Saf yeast

Place all the ingredients into the baking pan in the order listed. Bake. Cool on a rack.

MILLET TACO BREAD

1¼	cups + 1 Tablespoon water	2	Tablespoons gluten
2	Tablespoons honey	2	Tablespoons wheat bran
2	Tablespoons dry buttermilk powder	2	Tablespoons taco seasoning
2	Tablespoons oil	½	cup whole wheat flour
¾	teaspoon salt	2	cups bread flour
		2	teaspoons Saf yeast

Place all the ingredients into the baking pan in the order listed. Bake. Cool on a rack.

MOLASSES WALNUT BREAD

1	cup water	2	Tablespoons gluten
1	egg	2	teaspoons ground ginger
2	Tablespoons maple syrup or honey	¼	cup whole wheat flour
¾	teaspoon salt	2⅞	cups bread flour
2	Tablespoons molasses	2	teaspoons Saf yeast
1	Tablespoon oil	⅓	cup chopped walnuts

Place all the ingredients into the baking pan in the order listed. Bake. Cool on a rack.

NATURES BOUNTY-BEANS AND GARLIC BREAD

¾	cup baked bean puree	1	Tablespoon gluten
¾	cup water + 1 Tablespoon	2	Tablespoons wheat germ
2	Tablespoons oil	¼	cup mixed cereal flakes
½	teaspoon salt	1½	cups whole wheat flour
1	Tablespoon vinegar	1½	cups bread flour
1	crushed garlic clove	2	teaspoons Saf yeast

Place all the ingredients into the baking pan in the order listed. Bake. Cool on a rack.

NORTH DAKOTA MILLET BREAD

1	cup water	1	Tablespoon gluten
1	large egg	1	Tablespoon dry onion
½	cup cooked millet	¼	cup amaranth flour
2	Tablespoons honey	¼	cup red lentil flour
1	teaspoon salt	1	Tablespoon oat bran
1½	Tablespoons oil	½	cup whole wheat flour
2	Tablespoons cooked crumbled bacon	2	cups bread flour
		2	teaspoons Saf yeast

Place all the ingredients into the baking pan in the order listed. Bake. Cool on a rack.

OAT BRAN APRICOT PRUNE BREAD

1	cup water	¼	cup oat bran
3	Tablespoons dry buttermilk	¼	cup red lentil flour
1	egg	2	Tablespoons gluten
2	Tablespoons honey	¼	cup snipped dried apricots
1	teaspoon salt	¼	cup dried prunes, cut
1½	Tablespoons oil	2½	cups bread flour +1 Tablespoon
		2	teaspoons Saf yeast

Place all the ingredients into the baking pan in the order listed. Bake. Cool on a rack.

OATMEAL FRUIT BREAD

1	cup water	2	Tablespoons gluten
⅓	cup diced orange	¾	cup oatmeal
1½	Tablespoons oil	2	Tablespoons wheat germ
1	teaspoon salt	2¼	cups bread flour
1	Tablespoon lemon juice	½	cup snipped dried apricots
2½	Tablespoons honey		or other dried fruit
1	Tablespoon orange zest	¼	cup slivered almonds
		2	teaspoons Saf yeast

Place all the ingredients into the baking pan in the order listed. Bake. Cool on a rack.

ONION 'N HERB BREAD

1¼	cups milk	2	Tablespoons bran
1	Tablespoon sugar	¼	teaspoon crushed basil
1	teaspoon salt	2	Tablespoons gluten
1½	Tablespoons oil	⅛	teaspoon white pepper
1	teaspoon garlic powder	3	cups bread flour
½	teaspoon dill weed	1	Tablespoon lemon juice
1	teaspoon rosemary	2	teaspoons Saf yeast

Place all the ingredients into the baking pan in the order listed. Bake. Cool on a rack.

PEPPER CHEESE BREAD

1¼	cups water	2	Tablespoons tofu powder
2	Tablespoons dry buttermilk powder	1	Tablespoon gluten
2	Tablespoons sugar	2	teaspoons diced, mild chili peppers
1	teaspoon salt	3	cups bread flour
1½	Tablespoons oil	⅓	cup grated jalapeno pepper cheese
2	Tablespoons roasted, red pepper chopped	2	teaspoons Saf yeast

Place all the ingredients into the baking pan in the order listed. Bake. Cool on a rack.

PIZZA BREAD

½	cup water	2	Tablespoons pizza seasoning
½	cup tomato juice	½	cup whole wheat flour
1	egg	1½	cups bread flour
2	Tablespoons sugar	1	Tablespoon gluten
½	teaspoon salt	½	cup grated sharp cheddar cheese
1½	Tablespoons oil	2	teaspoons Saf yeast

Place all the ingredients into the baking pan in the order listed. Bake. Cool on a rack.

PIONEER BREAD

½	cup water	¼	cup mixed cereal
¾	cup milk	2	Tablespoons gluten
2	Tablespoons sugar	2	Tablespoons yellow lentil flour
1	teaspoon salt	2	Tablespoons wheat bran
2	teaspoons lemon juice	1	Tablespoon flax seed
1½	Tablespoons oil	2	cups bread flour
2	Tablespoons corn flour	½	cup whole wheat flour
		2	teaspoons Saf yeast

Place all the ingredients into the baking pan in the order listed. Bake. Cool on a rack.

PROVOLONE DRIED OLIVES AND HERBS BREAD

1¼	cups water plus 2 teaspoons	1	Tablespoon gluten
3	Tablespoons dry buttermilk powder	1	cup whole wheat flour
1	Tablespoon honey	2	cups bread flour
1	Tablespoon Greek herbs	2	Tablespoons sunflower seeds
1	teaspoon salt	¼	cup chopped dried olives
1½	Tablespoons oil	½	cup grated Provolone cheese
		2	teaspoons Saf yeast

Place all the ingredients into the baking pan in the order listed. Bake. Cool on a rack.

PURPLE SAGE POTATO BREAD

1	cup potato water including	2	Tablespoons cottage cheese
	¼ cup potato	2	Tablespoons oat bran
½	cup steamed tomato minus seeds	8	large fresh leaves purple sage, chopped
2	Tablespoons sugar		
2	Tablespoons oil	1	cup whole wheat flour
1	teaspoon salt	2	cups bread flour
1	Tablespoon dry onion flakes	2	teaspoons Saf yeast

Place all the ingredients into the baking pan in the order listed. Bake. Cool on a rack.

ROASTED SWEET RED PEPPER BASIL BREAD

1¼	cups water	⅛	teaspoon cayenne pepper
1	Tablespoon honey	1	Tablespoon gluten
1	teaspoon salt	1½	teaspoons sweet basil
1	Tablespoon tofu powder	3	cups bread flour
3	Tablespoons cottage cheese. mashed	2	teaspoons Saf yeast
½	teaspoon garlic flakes	3	Tablespoons chunked, roasted red pepper

Place all the ingredients into the baking pan in the order listed. Bake. Cool on a rack.

RUM NUT BREAD

1	cup water minus 2 Tablespoons	3	Tablespoons dry milk
2	Tablespoons rum	¼	cup oatmeal flakes
1	teaspoon salt	¼	cup whole wheat flour
1	Tablespoon brown sugar	2¾	cups bread flour
2	Tablespoons butter	2	teaspoons Saf yeast
2	Tablespoons plain yogurt	⅓	cup slivered almonds

Place all the ingredients into the baking pan in the order listed. Bake. Cool on a rack.

RYE 'N CARAWAY SEEDS BREAD

½	cup water	1	teaspoon salt
½	cup buttermilk	¼	teaspoon ginger
1½	Tablespoons sugar	2	Tablespoons gluten
3	Tablespoons molasses	1	cup rye flour
2	teaspoons caraway seeds	2	Tablespoons corn flour
2	teaspoons anise seeds	2	cups bread flour
1½	Tablespoons oil	2	teaspoons Saf yeast

Place all the ingredients into the baking pan in the order listed. Bake. Cool on a rack.

SAVORY COLONIAL BREAD WITH FRIED GREEN TOMATOES

1	cup water + 1 Tablespoon	2	teaspoon ground sage
3	Tablespoons dry buttermilk	2	Tablespoons gluten
2	Tablespoons sugar	¼	cup rye cereal flakes
1	teaspoon salt	2	Tablespoons yellow split pea flour
1½	Tablespoons oil		
⅓	cup chopped fried green tomatoes	1	cup whole wheat flour
2	Tablespoons corn flour	1¾	cups bread flour
		2	teaspoons Saf yeast

Place all the ingredients into the baking pan in the order listed. Bake. Cool on a rack.

SNOW WHITE AND THE SEVEN ODD FELLOWS BREAD

1	cup milk	2	Tablespoons potato flour
1	egg	2	Tablespoons tofu powder
¼	cup cooked millet	1	Tablespoon gluten
¾	teaspoon salt	2	Tablespoons brown rice flour
2	Tablespoons honey	2½	cups bread flour, plus 4½ Tablespoons
2	Tablespoons butter		
2	Tablespoons plain yogurt	2	teaspoons Saf yeast

Place all the ingredients into the baking pan in the order listed. Bake. Cool on a rack.

SPELT SUN-DRIED TOMATO BREAD

1½	cups water	3	Tablespoons gluten
3	Tablespoons dry buttermilk	3	Tablespoons sun-dried tomatoes, chopped
2	Tablespoons honey		
1	Tablespoon lemon juice	3⅓	cups spelt flour
1	teaspoon salt	⅓	cup bread flour plus 1 Tablespoon
⅓	cup chopped fried green tomatoes		
2	Tablespoons oil	2	teaspoons Saf yeast

Place all the ingredients into the baking pan in the order listed. Bake. Cool on a rack.

SUN-DRIED TOMATO PARMESAN CHEESE BREAD

½	cup water	1	Tablespoon tofu powder
½	cup buttermilk	⅓	cup whole wheat flour
1	egg	2⅔	cups bread flour, plus 2 Tablespoons
1½	Tablespoons sugar		
1	teaspoon salt	2	teaspoons Saf yeast
2	Tablespoons gluten	¼	cup Parmesan cheese, grated
1½	Tablespoons oil	3	Tablespoons chunked sun-dried tomatoes

Place all the ingredients into the baking pan in the order listed. Bake. Cool on a rack.

TRITICALE SUNFLOWER SEED BREAD

1	cup water	2	Tablespoons sunflower seeds
2	Tablespoons dry buttermilk	1	Tablespoon gluten
1	egg	1	Tablespoon tofu powder
1½	Tablespoons oil	½	cup rye flour
2	Tablespoons honey	½	cup triticale flakes
1	teaspoon salt	2⅓	cups bread flour
		2	teaspoons Saf yeast

Place all the ingredients into the baking pan in the order listed. Bake. Cool on a rack.

WHOLE WHEAT CALIFORNIA SOUR-DO BREAD

1¼	cups water	2	Tablespoons molasses
3	Tablespoons California Sour-Do	2	Tablespoons gluten
2	Tablespoons honey	2	Tablespoons wheat germ
1½	Tablespoons oil	3	cups whole wheat flour
1	teaspoon salt	2	teaspoons Saf yeast
2	Tablespoons lemon juice		

Place all the ingredients into the baking pan in the order listed. Bake. Cool on a rack.

WHOLE WHEAT (100%) BREAD

1	cup water	2	Tablespoons potato flour
⅓	cup buttermilk	2	Tablespoons oil
1	Tablespoon lemon juice	2	Tablespoons gluten
3	Tablespoons molasses	3¼	cups whole wheat flour
1	teaspoon sugar	1	Tablespoon orange zest
1	teaspoon salt	2¼	teaspoons Saf yeast
		⅓	cup chopped walnuts

Place all the ingredients into the baking pan in the order listed. Bake. Cool on a rack.

BEAN BACON AND CHEDDAR LOAF

Note: This bread recipe has been adapted for the one and one-half pound bread machine loaf. For chunky bacon, partially freeze the slices, then dice, fry and drain before adding it to the bread. Broiled bacon will crumble very fine.

QUICK SETTING: MEDIUM   **YIELD:** One 1½ pound loaf

1 egg	1 Tablespoon blended oil
¾ cup warm water	½ cup grated Cheddar cheese
½ cup mashed baked beans	¼ teaspoon sea salt
5-6 strips lean bacon broiled and crumbled	3 cups + 3 Tablespoons bread flour
2 Tablespoons honey	2¼ teaspoons Saf yeast

Prepare the bacon. Place all ingredients into the baking pan in the order listed, or add the yeast after the flour. Insert the baking pan securely into the bread machine. Select the desired baking cycle.

When the bread is finished, remove the pan from the machine using pot holders. Remove the loaf from the pan. Cool on a rack.

CRANBERRY, YOGURT, CHERRY, BANANA BREAD

Note: This combination of ingredients is "hungry" for protein, just like your body. The live enzymes in the fresh cherries and the protein in the yogurt will partially predigest the gluten in the flour. Therefore, the batter may be a bit tacky. After the first beating cycle, lift the lid and touch the dough with the back of your fingers. If the dough clings to the fingers, or it adheres to the walls of the pan, sprinkle in flour, one Tablespoon at a time, until the dough is semi- firm and leaves the side of the pan when the next beating cycle begins.

BASIC WHITE BREAD SETTING: MEDIUM   **YIELD:** 1 Loaf

½ cup water	2 Tablespoons sugar or honey
¼ cup Bing cherries, dried	2¾ cups high-gluten flour
¼ cup dried cranberries	2 Tablespoons White Enrichment mix
½ cup ripe banana, mashed	
½ cup homemade plain yogurt	½ cup oatmeal
1 teaspoon sea salt	2½ teaspoons Saf yeast or Red Star Active dry yeast

(continued)

Blend the dried cranberries with the yogurt and set aside for 20 minutes. Place all ingredients into the baking pan in the order listed. Insert the baking pan securely into the bread machine. Select the desired baking cycle. When the bread is finished, remove the loaf from the pan. Cool on a rack.

HOMEMADE FORTIFIED PLAIN YOGURT

    1   quart milk, whole raw, pasteurized, homogenized, nonfat,
        reconstituted skim milk, or soy milk
    ¼   cup nonfat non-instant dry milk Bulgarian yogurt culture

Blend the dry milk with the fresh milk. Heat to nearly boiling. Cool the milk to 100-115 degrees, checking with a dairy thermometer. Stir in the Bulgarian culture. Place the yogurt in sterilized jars and then into the yogurt maker. When finished, refrigerate.

Note: Red flame cherries (chopped) can substitute for Bing cherries.

"Learn to love Honor above all things."
Edna Lister

DILL CHEESE BREAD

Note: This high protein bread is very tender, with a faint fragrance of dill weed. It makes a perfect sandwich bread.

BASIC WHITE BREAD SETTING: MEDIUM   **YIELD:** One ½ pound loaf

½ cup water	¼ teaspoon ginger
¾ cup cottage cheese	2 cups Yeast Bread Mix
2 Tablespoons honey	1¼ cups bread flour
2 Tablespoons canola oil	1 teaspoon sea salt

Puree the cottage cheese with the water. Place all ingredients in the baking pan in the order listed, or add the yeast after the flour. Insert the baking pan securely into the bread machine. Select the desired baking cycle.

When the bread is finished, remove the pan from the machine using pot holders. Remove the loaf from the pan. Cool on a rack.

Note: You can make a zesty loaf by adding 2 Tablespoons grated Romano cheese and 1 Tablespoon dry onion flakes. Use the "Light" setting on the machine if you add Romano cheese.

HONEY APPLE NUT BREAD

RAISIN BREAD SETTING: LIGHT CRUST   **YIELD:** 1 loaf

Soak ⅓ cup raisins for 10-15 minutes in 1 cup warm water. Chop lightly in the blender. Use the raisins and water for the liquid.

1 cup raisin water	2 Tablespoons soy milk powder
2 Tablespoons frozen apple juice concenrate	2½ cups high gluten flour
1½ Tablespoons blended oil, or butter	½ cup whole wheat flour
1 teaspoon sea salt	2 teaspoons Saf yeast
	⅓ cup walnuts, chopped

Add the ingredients, except the walnuts and raisins, into the baking pan in the order listed, or add the yeast after the flour. Insert the baking pan securely into the bread machine. Select the desired baking cycle.
When the bread is finished, remove the pan from the machine using pot holders. Remove the loaf from the pan. Cool on a rack.

NOTE: If the raisins are not soaked, add 1 Tablespoon sugar or honey to the recipe. Nonfat dry milk may be substituted for the powdered soy milk.

JACK'S CONEY ISLAND BREAD

Brooklyn has nothing on the Puget Sound Area. We have amusement parks, islands, hot dogs and the fresh garden tomatoes for creating Coney Island Sauce. All we need to do is to whip up a wholesome loaf of bread. With this quick recipe, even the hot dog part is simple.

BASIC WHITE BREAD SETTING: MEDIUM   **YIELD:** 1 large loaf

¾ cup water	½-1 teaspoon sea salt
2 teaspoons Saf yeast	1½ Tablespoons lecithin
2 Tablespoons sugar	butter or oil
1 cup sharp	½ cup salsa sauce, medium
Cheddar cheese, grated	3½ cups bread flour

Measure the ingredients into the baking pan, "in reverse order," says my friend Dottie, from Dottie's Bosch Kitchen in Puyallup, Washington. "It keeps the baking pan clean." Add yeast last.

Select the desired baking cycle. When the bread is finished, remove the pan from the machine using pot holders. Remove the loaf from the pan. Cool on a rack.

NOTE: Add only 3¼ cups flour to begin the process. After the bread begins to mix, open the lid and check the dough. If the dough is sticky to the touch, add 1 Tablespoon of flour at a time during the mixing process, until the dough becomes slightly firm to the touch.

KAMUT AND WHEAT BREAD

BASIC WHITE BREAD SETTING: MEDIUM   **YIELD:** 1 large loaf

1 cup potato water	1 large egg
or buttermilk	¾ teaspoon sea salt
1½ Tablespoons blended oil	¾ cup Kamut flour
2 Tablespoon sugar,	2⅞ cups high-gluten flour
or honey	2¼ teaspoons Saf yeast,
	or Red Star active yeast

Measure the ingredients into the baking pan. Insert the baking pan into the machine securely. Select the settings. Open the lid after the mixing begins. If the dough is tacky, add 1 Tablespoon of flour at a time until the dough can be lightly touched without sticking to fingers. When the bread is completed, remove the loaf from the pan. Cool on a rack.

Note: ⅞ cup whole wheat flour may be substituted for 1 cup bread flour.

PEAR ZUCCHINI BREAD

Note: Here in the Pacific Northwest, where fruit and vegetables abound, it's easy to become an improvisational cook. For the most part, the yield in my yard is so heavy I have to create new recipes to use up the excess produce. When the fruit and vegetables top the amount that my family and friends can use, we give the extra to the needy.

BASIC WHITE BREAD SETTING: MEDIUM   **YIELD** 1 Large Loaf

½ cup milk	1 teaspoon sea salt
¾ cup pear/zucchini puree	2 cups Yeast Bread Mix
2 Tablespoons sugar	2 teaspoons
⅛ teaspoon ginger	orange peel, grated
2 Tablespoons sesame oil	1½ cups bread flour
	3 Tablespoons walnuts, chopped

Place all ingredients into the baking pan in the order listed. Insert the baking pan securely into the bread machine. Select the desired baking cycle.

When the bread is finished, remove the pan from the machine using pot holders. Remove the loaf from the pan. Cool on a rack.

PEAR-ZUCCHINI PUREE

¼ cup pear juice	1 pear, canned
1 small zucchini, cubed	

Peel and dice the zucchini. Drain the canned pears. Heat ¼ cup pear juice. Add the zucchini cubes. Steam until soft. Add the pear and zucchini to the blender. Use the pulse setting to blend the mixture. Measure out ½ cup for the recipe. Freeze the remainder in a sealed container or add it to cooked winter squash.

Note: Three-Grain Bread Mix may be substituted for Yeast Bread Mix.

Food Safety:
If bread dough or breads are frozen, they must be thawed under refrigeration; particularly if the product contains meat or eggs.

PINEAPPLE SPELT BREAD

Note: Keep in mind that bread machines are predominantly programmed for wheat flour. Therefore, when a recipe calls for other grains, you have to experiment a bit with the settings. The finer-grind spelt flour is used for this loaf. Spelt is a heavier grain than wheat and yields a soft, smooth loaf. Spelt makes a wonderful addition to the daily diet because it is high in protein, iron, potassium, complex carbohydrates and contains many other beneficial nutrients. Finally, people with food allergies may be able to eat this bread without difficulty.

BASIC WHITE BREAD SETTING: LIGHT   **YIELD:** 1 loaf

1 cup canned pineapple juice	1 cup high-gluten flour
1 Tablespoon sugar	1 Tablespoon soy flour
1 teaspoon sea salt	2 teaspoons Saf yeast
2¼ cups spelt flour	⅛ teaspoon ground ginger

Place all ingredients into the baking pan in the order listed. Insert the baking pan securely into the bread machine. Select the desired baking cycle. When the bread is finished, remove the pan from the machine using pot holders. Remove the loaf from the pan. Cool on a rack.

Note: The flour must be spoon-dipped into the measuring cup, not dipped. All ingredients must be measured level for best results. The "medium" bake setting is good for those who like a snappy crust on their loaf of bread.

Tip: The baking pan can be lifted from the machine nicely by using the dough hook from a bread mixer. Contrary to popular belief or advice given by some cooks, bread pans do need to be washed and scalded between bakings, for food safety reasons.

Tip: When soy products or honey are added to a recipe, the product will brown more rapidly during the baking process.

Tip: Dark rye bread can be re-cycled into sourdough starters.
4 cups rye bread cubes, ¼ cup plain yogurt, 3½-4 cups warm water, ½ teaspoon dry yeast, 1 teaspoon sugar and ¼ cup rye flour. Cover. Let ferment. Use like other sourdough starters.

PIZZA BREAD

BASIC WHITE BREAD SETTING: **YIELD:** 1 loaf
DOUGH SETTING FOR PIZZAS: MEDIUM CRUST

1 cup water	2 Tablespoons soy milk powder
¼ cup tomato juice	2¼ cups high-gluten flour
1 Tablespoon sugar	1¼ cup whole wheat flour
2 Tablespoons blended oil, or butter	2 teaspoons pizza seasoning
¾ teasoon sea salt	1 Tablespoon dry onion flakes
	2¼ teaspoons instant dry yeast

Add the ingredients to the baking pan in the order listed. When the bread is finished, remove from the pan. Cool on a rack.

For pizza crusts, use the "Dough" setting. When the machine beeps, remove the dough from the pan. Form a loaf. Place it in a prepared pan. Cover and let rise until nearly doubled in bulk. Bake 400 degrees for 30-35 minutes. Cool on a rack.

Fill with the family favorite pizza foods and sauces. Bake in the oven at 450 degrees for 15 minutes. Add a cheese topping and bake 5-6 minutes longer.

Old Fashioned Easter Egg Coloring Tips:
When we celebrated Easter Sunday in the country, we wished for new clothes and "real" coloring for making Easter eggs. In those days of poverty, we dunked our eggs in boiling black coffee or Watkins vanilla. Some of the eggs were wrapped in wet crepe paper, others were dipped into beet juice from the pickled beets and in heated dandelion flowers or nasturtium blossom water.

POTATO BREAD

Note: See the general Baking Instructions in the front of this book for the Potato Water recipe.

BASIC WHITE BREAD SETTING: Medium   **YIELD:** 1 large loaf

1 cup Potato Water	1 Tablespoon soy milk, powder or nonfat dry milk
¼ cup buttermilk	¾ teaspoon sea salt
1 Tablespoon sugar, or honey	3¼ cups high-gluten flour
1½ Tablespoon blended oil	$2\frac{1}{8}$ teaspoons Saf dry yeast, or Red Star active yeast

Place all ingredients into the baking pan in the order listed. Insert the baking pan securely into the bread machine. Select the desired baking cycle.

When the bread is finished, remove the pan from the machine using pot holders. Remove the loaf from the pan. Cool on a rack.

POTTAGE POTATO BREAD

BASIC WHITE BREAD SETTING: MEDIUM   **YIELD:** 1 loaf

⅓ cup Pottage Potato Mix	1 teaspoon lecithin butter
1 cup + 2 Tablespoons milk	⅓ cup whole wheat flour
2 Tablespoons honey	3 cups bread flour
1 teaspoon sea salt	2 teaspoons Saf yeast

Place all ingredients into the baking pan in the order listed. Insert the baking pan securely into the bread machine. Select the desired baking cycle. When the bread is finished, remove the pan from the machine using pot holders. Remove the loaf from the pan. Cool on a rack.

Note: Pottage & Potato Mix—cook together ¼ cup lentils and 1 small potato in 1½ cups water. Mash together.

"Life must be faced, not evaded."
Edna Lister

PRUNE NUT YEAST BREAD

RAISIN BREAD SETTING: MEDIUM   **YIELD:** 1 loaf

¾ cup milk	1 Tablespoon oil
½ cup prune puree	2 cups Yeast Bread Mix
1 medium egg	1¼ cups bread flour
⅔ teaspoon sea salt	⅓ cup walnuts, chopped

Place all ingredients into the baking pan in the order listed, or add the yeast after the flour. Insert the baking pan securely into the bread machine. Select the desired baking cycle.

When the bread is finished, remove the pan from the machine using pot holders. Remove the loaf from the pan. Cool on a rack.

RYE BREAD, LARGE LOAF

Note: This whole grain rye bread mix can be used in the bread machine or in an electric mixer. Either method will turn out a batch of a lighter, fluffier, more flavorful rye bread than you imagine. ENJOY!

BASIC WHITE BREAD SETTING: MEDIUM   **YIELD:** 1 loaf

1 large egg	¼ cup dark molasses
1 cup warm water	¼ cup bread flour
2 Tablespoons blended oil	3⅔ cups Rye Bread Mix
2 teaspoons cocoa	¼ cup sunflower seeds
½ teaspoon allspice	1 Tablespoon caraway
2 teaspoons orange zest	seeds, optional

Measure all ingredients into the baking pan in the order listed. Insert the baking pan securely into the bread machine. Select the desired baking cycle.

When the bread is finished, remove the pan from the machine using pot holders. Remove the loaf from the pan. Cool on a rack.

SAVORY BEAN AND BACON BREAD

Note: This recipe can be made with either home baked beans or canned beans. The bacon must be broiled and well drained. The addition of bacon gives a hint of the aroma and flavor of open campfire cooking. The bread is excellent for sandwiches,toast, or croustades.

RAISIN BREAD SETTING: MEDIUM   **YIELD:** 1 loaf

½ cup baked beans, pureed	2 Tablespoons lecithin butter
¾ cup water	1½ cups Yeast Bread Mix
1 egg	2½ cups bread flour
6-8 slices broiled bacon, crumbled	

Measure into the baking pan all ingredients in the order listed, except the bacon. Insert the baking pan securely into the unit; close the lid. Select the bake settings. The "beep" will sound after approximately 30 minutes. Add the crumbled bacon. Close the lid. The "COMPLETE" light will flash when the bread is done. Remove the pan with hotpads. Cool bread on a rack.

SAVORY SOUP STOCK BREAD

BASIC WHITE BREAD SETTING: MEDIUM   **YIELD:** 1 loaf

1 cup meat/vegetable stock, strained	2 Tablespoons lecithin butter
1 medium egg	2¼ cups Yeast Bread Mix
	2 cups bread flour

Measure all ingredients into the baking pan in the order listed. Insert the baking pan securely into the bread machine. Select the desired baking cycle.

When the bread is finished, remove the pan from the machine using pot holders. Remove the loaf from the pan. Cool on a rack.

"To believe that one cannot do a thing is a way to make it impossible."
Edna Lister

SPROUTED WHEAT

Note: For home sprouting, purchase seeds that have not been treated with fungicides or preservatives. Choose only seeds that are kept under refrigeration. Seeds are rich in many vitamins and minerals, and sprouts are one of the cheapest sources of natural vitamins and minerals you can find. Cooking, however, does reduce the potency of some nutrients.

RAISIN BREAD SETTING: MEDIUM   **YIELD:** 1 loaf

1¼ cups water	1 cup whole wheat flour
1 Tablespoon honey	2 cups Yeast Bread Mix
2 Tablespoons canola oil	1 cup bread flour
½ teaspoon sea salt	⅔ cup sprouts, or chopped nuts

Measure all ingredients into the baking pan in the order listed. Insert the baking pan securely into the bread machine. Select the desired baking cycle.

When the bread is finished, remove the pan from the machine using pot holders. Remove the loaf from the pan. Cool on a rack.

SPROUTING SEEDS

Everyone has their own favorite method of sprouting seeds. Here is one simple method:

1. Soak the seeds overnight. Drain.

2. Place a paper towel in the bottom of a colander, THEN scatter the seeds on the towel.

3. Place another paper towel over the top. Rinse under running water. Set aside.

4. Rinse twice daily.

5. When the sprouts reach twice the length of the seed, the sprouts are ready to use.
   Rinse and refrigerate.

Tip: Add alfalfa sprouts, or other cereal grain sprouts, (in pureed form), to salad dressing blends, gravies and baked potato toppings.

TOFU PEPPER BREAD

BASIC WHITE BREAD SETTING: MEDIUM   **YIELD:** 1 loaf

¼-½ teaspoon pepper flakes	1 teaspoon sea salt
½ cup milk	2 Tablespoons sesame
+2 Tablespoons milk	seed oil
¼ cup tofu, mashed	2 cups Three Grain Bread Mix
2 Tablespoons sugar	1¼ cups bread Flour
	¼ cup Parmesan, or
	Romano cheese, grated

Measure the ingredients into the baking pan in the order shown. Insert the baking pan securely into the machine. Select the baking settings above. The light will flash when the bread is finished. Using hot pads, remove the baking pan from the machine. Cool the bread on a rack.

"Endurance is FAITH tried almost to the breaking point."
God Calling Devotional

WILD RICE AND BUCKWHEAT BREAD

Note: Because buckwheat is a non-gluten grain, it must be accompanied by wheat or another gluten source to make the bread rise. This grain is an excellent source of minerals and trace minerals.

DOUGH SETTING: Medium   **YIELD:** 1 loaf

1¼ cups milk	¼ cup buckwheat flour
1 medium egg	2 Tablespoons gluten
2 Tablespoons canola oil	2½ cups bread flour,
½ teaspoon sea salt	or unbleached white flour
¼ cup wild rice flour	1 Tablespoon instant
	dry yeast

Note: Follow bread machine instructions for dough setting.

Buckwheat is high in the mineral magnesium. It has a good amount of copper, chromium and manganese, along with small amounts of iron and selenium. Consider adding small amounts of buckwheat to other recipes.

YOGURT DILL BREAD

Note: If the bread mix has been stored in the freezer, bring it to room temperature before beginning the bread making procedure.

BASIC WHITE BREAD SETTING: MEDIUM   **YIELD:** 1 loaf

$^7/_8$ cup plain yogurt	1½ cups Yeast Bread Mix
1 large egg	2¼ cups bread flour, or
2 Tablespoons canola oil	2¼ cups unbleached white
¼ teaspoon sea salt	flour +1 Tablespoon gluten
2¼ teaspoons dill weed	

Measure all ingredients into the baking pan in the order listed. Insert the baking pan securely into the bread machine. Select the desired baking cycle.

When the bread is finished, remove the pan from the machine using pot holders. Remove the loaf from the pan. Cool on a rack.

Note: $^7/_8$ cup = 1 cup minus 2 Tablespoons

DILL AND MILLET LOAF

BASIC WHITE SETTING: MEDIUM   **YIELD:** 1 Loaf

1¼ cup buttermilk	3 Tablespoon cooked millet
2 Tablespoons sunflower seed oil	1 Tablespoon cornmeal
1½ Tablespoons honey	⅔ cup millet flour
2 teaspoons dill weed	1 cup whole wheat flour
500 milligrams vitamin C	2 cups bread flour
1 teaspoon sea salt	1 Tablespoon instant yeast or
	2 teaspoons Red Star yeast

Place all ingredients into the baking pan in the order listed, or add the yeast after the flour. Insert the baking pan securely into the bread machine. Select the desired baking cycle.

When the bread is finished, remove the pan from the machine using pot holders. Remove the loaf from the pan. Cool on a rack.

"Being angry about things one does not understand is called fear".
Edna Lister

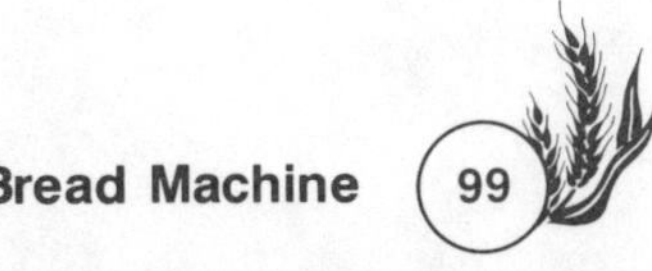

Bread Machine   99

QUICK ROLLS USING BREAD RECIPES

BASIC DINNER ROLLS

OVEN TIME: 20 minutes at 400 Degrees   **YIELD:** 16 dinner rolls

2 cups Basic Yeast
Convenience Mix
1¼ cups hot water, (120°)
2¼-3 cups bread flour

1½ Tablespoons blended oil
1 egg, beaten

Add the Bread Mix to a large bowl or electric mixer bowl. Stir in the hot water. Beat immediately for 1 minute. Stop the motor. Let the dough rest 10-20 minutes. Add the egg and oil. Beat 2 minutes. If beating by hand, beat 200 strokes. Gradually blend in the bread flour. Turn the dough out onto a sprinkling of flour. Knead well. Sprinkle more flour if needed to make a smooth and elastic dough. Cover. Let it rest for 20 minutes.

Pat the dough into a rectangle. Cut with a cookie cutter or a pizza cutter. (If you're cutting on the cabinet top instead of a bread board, use a plastic pizza cutter.) Place the gem-size rolls on a greased baking sheet. Let rise slightly. Bake. Cool on a rack. The tops may be oiled for a softer crust.

Fantastic and Fancy Dinner Roll Shapes:
Roll the dough to ½-¾ inch thick. Cut 6-8 inch strips measuring ¾ inches wide. Grasp each end of the strip and twist in opposite directions. Brush with glaze. Let rise and bake.

Roll the dough to ¾ inch thick. Cut with a pizza cutter into diamond shapes. Round off the corners and snip down the center with kitchen shears, allowing the points to protrude. Glaze and sprinkle with a seed mixture.

Tip: Dried fruits and vegetables add color and flavor to all breads and dinner rolls. Add them later during the mixing process so they do not soak away the liquid used. (soaking will also change the color of the dough).

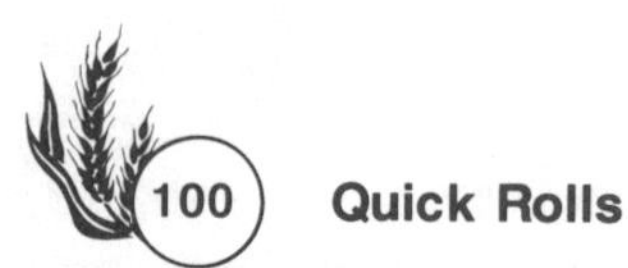

GARLIC CHEESE ROLLS

2 cups Basic Convenience Mix	½ cup Sharp Cheddar cheese, grated
1 cup hot water (120°)	1½ Tablespoons blended oil
1 egg	2-2½ cups bread flour, or, unbleached white flour
2 teaspoons garlic flakes	

Measure the basic mix into a large bowl or electric mixer bowl. Add the warm water. Start beating immediately. Beat 2 minutes. Scrape down the inside of the bowl. Beat in the oil, egg and garlic flakes. Add the grated cheese. Gradually beat in the flour. When the dough leaves the side of the bowl, turn it out onto a sprinkling of flour. Knead well. Press or roll the dough to fit a 13x9x2-inch oiled pan. Cut to desired size; brush the top of the dough with oil. Let rise and bake for 25-30 minutes at 400 degrees. Serve hot with Lecithin Butter.

> *"Learn to become that which you demand others to be."*
> *Edna Lister*

RYE AND CHEESE ROLLS

OVEN TIME: 20 minutes at 400 degrees   **YIELD:** 12-14 rolls

2½-3 cups rye bread mix	¾ cup Swiss cheese, grated
1 cup warm water	1½ Tablespoons blended oil
1 large egg	¼ cup bread flour
1 Tablespoon sunflower seeds	

Stir the Rye Mix and measure it into the electric mixer bowl. Add the warm water. Begin beating immediately. Beat 2 minutes. Scrape down the inside of the bowl. Beat in the oil, egg, sunflower seeds and cheese. Turn the dough out onto a sprinkling of flour and knead lightly. Press the dough into a 13x9x2 inch sprayed pan. Cut the dough into the desired roll size. Let rise until doubled in bulk. Brush with oil. Bake. When the rolls are finished, remove them from the pan. Cool on a rack.

> *"Miracles are not made by wavering, doubt or fear."*
> *Lotus Landis*

SOURDOUGH BREADS

GENERAL RULES FOR MAKING SOURDOUGH STARTERS
Glass or earthenware bowls are the best containers for making starters.
Add the ingredients to be fermented and whisk them together. Cover the
bowl with stretch plastic wrap. The wrap will sweat, forming droplets of
water that keep the ferment moist. Allow the mixture to remain at room
temperature overnight, or longer. The longer the mixture stands at room
temperature, the more sour it becomes. Once the desired sourness is
reached, pour the mixture into a jar, seal and refrigerate. As the mixture is
used, stir in added flour and liquid. Refrigerate.

SOURDOUGH STARTERS

AUNT EMMA'S "BIG BATCH" STARTER

5 medium potatoes	¼ cup sugar
5 cups water	3 Tablespoons whey powder
2 cups flour	1 Tablespoon instant
1 teaspoon sea salt	dry yeast
	½ teaspoon ground ginger

Scrub, cube and cook the potatoes in 2 cups of water. Mash the potatoes
in the cooking water. Remove from heat, then cool until warm to the touch.

In a large bowl, dissolve the yeast in 1 cup warm water and add the sugar.
Add the mashed potatoes and the remaining water. Blend in the remaining
ingredients. Whisk until smooth. Cover with a single thickness of
cheesecloth. Let rest at room temperature for 24 hours. This will allow wild
yeast to inhabit the mixture. Cover tightly with a clinging transparent wrap.
Stir the mixture 2 times daily. After 2 or 3 more days the mixture will
become light and foamy. Place it in a large jar. Seal and keep refrigerated.

Use 1 cup of the starter for each loaf of bread. When making a new batch
of starter, use one cup of the "old maid."

BUCKWHEAT SEMOLINA STARTER

1 cup warm water	¼ cup buckwheat flour
½ cup plain yogurt	¼ cup semolina flour
½ teaspoon instant dry yeast	1½ cups unbleached white flour

In a large china or enamel bowl, dissolve the yeast in warm water. Whisk in the remaining ingredients. Cover with one layer of cheese cloth and let stand at room temperature for 24 hours. Stir well. Cover tightly with clinging transparent wrap. Let stand at room temperature for 2-3 days. Stir the starter and pour it into a glass jar. Seal and refrigerate.

CORNMEAL POTATO STARTER

3 medium potatoes	½ teaspoon instant dry yeast
2½ cups water	2 teaspoons sugar
1 cup cornmeal	¼ teaspoon ground ginger
½ cup warm water	2 cups unbleached white flour

Scrub the potatoes well. Remove all blemishes and cube the potatoes. Cook the potatoes in 1½ cups of water. Stir in the cornmeal. Remove from the heat. Mash the potatoes in the cooking water with the cornmeal. Set aside. Cool until warm to the touch. Dissolve the yeast in the warm water and add the sugar.

Blend the potato mixture and yeast in a large glass or earthenware bowl. Whisk well. Blend the ginger with the flour and beat into the potato mixture. Scrape down the inside of the bowl. Cover with a light cheesecloth and let stand at room temperature for 24 hours.
Stir the mixture. Cover tightly with transparent clinging wrap. Let stand at room temperature for 2-3 days. When the starter is light and foamy, stir it again and place it in a sealed jar. Keep refrigerated.

HEAD START SOURDOUGH

1 cup plain yogurt	1 teaspoon sea salt
1 cup warm water	1 teaspoon sugar
1 medium potato, grated	3½ cups flour
¼ cup nonfat dry milk	

(Con't)

Sourdough Breads   103

In a large glass bowl or an earthenware bowl, stir the yogurt and warm water together. Add the remaining ingredients. Whisk to a smooth batter. Scrape down the inside of the bowl. Cover with one thickness of cheesecloth for 24 hours.

Stir the mixture and cover it tightly with clinging transparent wrap. Let the starter remain at room temperature for 2-3 more days, until thin and foamy. Place it in a sealed jar and keep refrigerated.

LILLIAN CARTER'S RAW POTATO STARTER

1¼ cups warm water	¾ cup raw potato, grated
¼ cup sour milk or yogurt	2 teaspoons white
1½ cups unbleached white flour	Karo syrup or honey
	1 teaspoon sea salt

Scrub the potato and remove all blemishes. Grate the potato and blend in the salt. (Don't worry about the flecks of potato peeling in the batter, the mixture will change color regardless due to the action of the raw potato during the fermenting process.)

In a medium-sized bowl, whisk the ingredients together. Cover lightly with a cloth or cheesecloth. Set the container where it will collect wild yeast spores from the air. (Mamma set her starter out of doors in the shade.) Let it work for 24 hours, or longer. Cover the container tightly with transparent wrap. Stir the mixture once a day. Scrape the inside of the bowl before covering.

Do not allow the mixture to remain at a temperature above 80 degrees, or it may spoil. Store the liquid in a sealed jar. When ½ to 1 inch of liquid works to the top, it is ready to use. To restore the mixture, whisk back into the starter equal parts of water and flour for each 2 cups removed for baking, plus ⅛ teaspoon sugar. Keep the remaining mixture at 2 cups.

 Sourdough Breads

RAW POTATO SOURDOUGH BREAD

Note: Our thanks to Sir Francis Drake (1577) and Sir Walter Raleigh (1588) for the discovery of the humble potato. The Irish potato apparently originated in the Chilean area of South America. My family of 14 survived because the climate and soil of North Dakota were conducive for growing potato crops. Many people do not realize that the potato contains many valuable nutrients: 12 amino acids, some 20 minerals, organic acids, enzymes, pectin and vitamin C. That should be enough reason for you to incorporate this easy-to-grow and economical food into your daily diet.

OVEN TIME: 30-35 minutes at 400 degrees   **YIELD:** 1 loaf

1 cup warm water	2 teaspons sea salt
1 teaspoon Saf yeast	2 Tablespoons gluten
1 cup sourdough starter	2 cups bread flour
2 Tablespoons honey	2-2½ cups whole wheat flour

In a large bowl or electric mixer bowl, dissolve the yeast in the warm water and add the honey. Add the potato sourdough starter. Blend. In a small bowl mix the gluten with 2 cups flour. Gradually add it to the batter. Beat after each addition. Scrape down the inside of the bowl. Add the sea salt and oil. Beat to blend.

Gradually add the remaining flour. Beat after each addition. When the dough begins to leave the side of the bowl, turn it out on a flat surface onto a sprinkling of flour. Knead until the dough becomes smooth and elastic. Place it in an oiled bowl. Turn to coat all sides. Cover. Let rise until doubled in bulk. Punch the dough down. Turn out on a flat surface and press out the remaining air bubbles. Let rest for 3-4 minutes.

Form a large loaf or two small loaves. Place in prepared pans. Cover. Let rise until nearly doubled. Brush the top with oil, or egg white mixed with 1 Tablespoon water. Bake. When the loaves are finished, remove from the pans. Cool on a rack.

Tip: French bread can be brushed with a mixture of 3 Tablespoons warm water, ½ teaspoon active yeast (to the dissolved bubbly stage). Stir in 2 Tablespoons cracked millet or bulgur wheat. Let stand 10 minutes. Brush bread half way into baking cycle.

SOURDOUGH FRENCH BREAD

The tang of sourdough seems to tempt everyone's palate, particularly when it's served with a spaghetti dinner, or just a picnic in the back yard. This bread is made with Lillian's Raw Potato Sourdough Starter. French bread can be brushed with water at intervals while baking. Omit the seed garnish if you plan to brush the loaf.

OVEN TIME: 5 minutes at 425 degrees
20 minutes at 375 degrees

YIELD: 2 long loaves

1½ cups Lillian's sourdough starter	1 teaspoon sea salt
1 Tablespoon sugar	1 cup whole wheat flour
½ cup warm water	½ cup Enrichment Mix
1 teaspoon Saf yeast	3½-4 cups high-gluten flour
⅓ cup apple juice	2 egg whites
¾ teaspoon garlic powder	poppy or sesame seeds

In an electric mixer bowl, dissolve the yeast in the warm water and apple juice. Add the sugar. Add the sourdough starter and 2 cups flour. Beat 2 minutes. If time allows, let the mixture rest for 10 minutes. In a separate bowl, blend the garlic powder, Enrichment Mix, sea salt, and whole wheat flour. (Reserve the remaining white flour.) Add 1 cup to the batter and beat 2 minutes. Beat the egg whites until stiff, but not dry. Fold into the batter by hand. Add remaining white flour. Blend well. Turn the dough out onto a sprinkling of flour and knead until smooth and elastic. Add sprinkles of flour as needed.

Form a ball of the dough. Place it in an oiled bowl. Turn to coat all sides. Cover and let rise until doubled in bulk. Punch down. Let rise a second time (for a finer texture), if time permits. Turn the dough out on a flat surface. Press out the remaining air bubbles. Divide the dough. To form the loaves, roll each piece into a rectangle approximately 9x20 for thin loaves, or 11x17 for a fatter loaf. Cover and let rise until nearly doubled in bulk.

Make diagonal slits in the top of the loaf. Brush the loaf with a mixture of 1 egg white and 2 Tablespoons water, whisked together. For darker shiny crust, brush with 1 egg yolk, whisked in 1½ Tablespoons water. Sprinkle with poppy seeds or sesame seeds. Bake the loaves with a pan of water in the oven, or toss 2-3 ice cubes on the floor of the oven. Bake. (Don't forget to reduce the heat after 5 minutes.) When the loaf is finished, remove it from the pan. Cool on a rack.

 Sourdough Breads

SOURDOUGH ONION BREAD

Note: This recipe makes an excellent party bread, a quick pizza-style lunch, or an accompaniment to spaghetti.

OVEN TIME: 30-35 minutes at 425 degrees   **YIELD:** 2 loaves

2 cups boiling water	2 teaspoons sea salt
¼ cup cornmeal	2 egg whites, beaten
2 Tablespoons onion, diced or dry onion soup mix	3 cups bread flour, or all-purpose flour
2 teaspoons instant dry yeast	3½-4 cups whole wheat flour
1 Tablespoon sugar	1 egg white
2 cups Head Start sourdough	

In a small saucepan, bring the water to a boil. Sprinkle in the cornmeal. Add the onion or soup mix. Stir and remove from the heat. Transfer the mixture into an electric mixer bowl. Cool until warm to the touch. Stir in the yeast and sugar. When the yeast is dissolved, add the sourdough and stir to blend. Add the white flour. Beat 2 minutes. Add the sea salt and fold in the beaten egg whites.

Gradually add the remaining flour. When the dough begins to climb the dough hook, turn it out on a flat surface onto a sprinkling of flour. Knead well. Place the dough in an oiled bowl. Turn to coat all sides. Cover. Let rise until doubled in bulk.

Knead the dough down. Turn out on a flat surface. Press out the remaining air bubbles. Divide the dough. Let it rest for 10 minutes. Form the loaves. Place on oiled baking sheets, or in baguettes. Cover. Let rise until nearly doubled in bulk. Brush the top of the loaves with a mixture of 1 egg white and 2 Tablespoons water. Bake. When the loaf is finished, remove it from the pan. Cool on a rack.

"Skirmishes of the heart, be they physical or emotional, can be prevented with applied nutrition and with the application of continual happy and positive thoughts."
Ferne Chapman

SOUR-DO RYE MOCK BEER BREAD

Note: This whole grain rye bread is made using the Rye Bread Mix. The mix can be used in the bread machine or an electric mixer. The bread has a delicious, old-country malted rye flavor.

OVEN TIME: 5 minutes at 425 degrees　　**YIELD:** 2 round domes
20-25 minutes at 375 degrees

2¼ cups hot water	3 Tablespoons California Sour-Do
1 cup rye flakes	1 teaspoon ground ginger
4 cups Rye Bread Mix	1 Tablespoon orange zest
¼-½ cup high gluten-flour	3 Tablespoons sunflower seeds
¼ cup molasses or malt flavor	
¼ teaspoon ground allspice	

In an electric mixer bowl, pour the hot water over the rye flakes. Immediately begin to beat in the Rye Bread Mix. Add the malt or molasses.

Blend together the California Sour-Do and spices. Add and beat 2 minutes. Add the sunflower seeds. Scrape down the inside of the bowl. When the dough begins to leave the side of the bowl, turn it out onto a sprinkling of flour. Knead until the dough is smooth and elastic. Place the dough in an oiled bowl, turn to oil all sides. Cover with wax paper and a cloth. Let rise until doubled in bulk.

Punch the dough down. Let rise again, if time permits. Let the dough rest for 5-10 minutes. Divide and form the loaves. Place in prepared round pans, or free-form on a baking sheet that has been dusted with cornmeal. With a sharp knife, cut a slash, or cross-shape in the tops of the loaves, about ¼ inch deep. Cover and let rise until nearly doubled in bulk. Bake. Loaves may be brushed with water two or three times while baking for a snappy crust. When the loaves are finished, remove from the pans. Cool on a rack.

Note: The loaves may be brushed with egg white whisked with 2 Tablespoons of water and sprinkled with sunflower seeds.

Tip: Nutritional yeast will not only heighten the malt flavor, but will add more nutrients to the bread.

BISCUITS

BISCUITS AND SCONE MIX

11 cups unbleached white flour
1 cup White Enrichment Mix
5 teaspoons sea salt

½ cup baking powder
½ cup sugar
Lecithin butter or shortening
to be added with the liquid
at the time of baking.

Stir-measure and add the ingredients to a large bowl. Stir to blend well.
Place in an airtight container. The mix is best kept under refrigeration. It
also freezes well.

COLONIAL BUTTERMILK BISCUITS

Note: The New England colonists were perhaps the originators of the maxim "make do or do without." However, this recipe is comparable to a true Southern biscuit. I have modified the recipe to improve its overall nutrition.

OVEN TIME: 12-15 minutes at 425 Degrees   **YIELD:** 24 biscuits

¾ cup unbleached white flour
1 cup whole wheat
pastry flour
¼ cup soy or oat flour
⅛ teaspoon sea salt
2 teaspoons baking powder
¾ cup buttermilk

1 Tablespoon sugar
¼ cup butter
2 egg whites
1 egg yolk
2 Tablespoons buttermilk
powder or non fat milk

Heat the oven. Spray the baking sheet.
In a large bowl, combine the white flour, whole wheat pastry flour, soy
flour, salt, baking powder, sugar and buttermilk powder. Cut in the butter
with a pastry blender, or with two knives, until the mixture resembles
coarsely cracked grain. In a separate bowl, whisk the egg whites, the egg
yolk and buttermilk together. Make a well in the center of flour mixture.
Add the liquid. Stir only long enough to blend the ingredients.
Place the dough onto a sprinkling of flour and knead lightly. Roll the
dough to ½ inch thick. Cut with a 2 inch biscuit cutter. Place on baking
sheets. Brush the tops with melted butter, if desired. Bake. Serve immediately, or cool on a rack.

SCONES OR BISCUITS

OVEN TIME: 12-15 minutes at 450 degrees   **YIELD:** 6-8 scones

2¼ cups Biscuit/Scone Mix ⅔ cup whole milk	⅓ cup shortening, butter, or lecithin butter

Heat the oven. In a large bowl, cut the shortening or butter into the dry ingredients. Add the liquid. Mix only enough to blend. Turn the dough out onto a sprinkling of flour. Knead lightly. Roll to ½-¾ inch thick.

Cut to desired size. Bake on an ungreased baking sheet. Cool on a rack.

Note: This recipe can be varied by adding ½ cup crushed pineapple while omitting ½ cup milk. ⅓ cup tomato juice can replace ⅓ cup of milk. Blend the remaining milk and the tomato juice before stirring into the biscuit mix. Add ½ cup grated sharp cheese to the mixture, after the liquid is added.

SCOTCH-STYLE SCONES

OVEN TIME: 12-15 minutes at 450 degrees   **YIELD:** 12 scones

3¼ cups unbleached flour 2 Tablespoons nonfat dry milk powder 1 Tablespoon + 2 teaspoons baking powder 2 Tablespoons soy powder, optional ¾ teaspoon salt	⅓ cup sugar ⅓ cup shortening or margarine 2 eggs ¾ cup whole milk or ½ cup evaporated milk + ¼ cup water

In a large bowl, blend first six ingredients. Cut in shortening or margarine. Separate one egg and set aside the white. Beat the second egg with the separated yolk and milk. Blend the milk mixture quickly into the dry ingredients. Turn dough out onto a lightly floured board. Divide dough into two equal portions. Form two equal rounds of dough approximately ½ inch thick.

Beat the remaining egg white. Brush each portion of dough with beaten egg white, and cut each into quarters. Place on greased cookie sheet. Bake. Serve hot with sweet cream butter and jam. Do not cut scones with a knife. Pull apart gently.

110   **Biscuits**

SELF-BUTTERED SCONES

Note: Each Fall at the Western Washington State Fair, one of the main attractions is the scone booth, where fresh baked scones, oozing with butter and jam, are served. (For Americans, these ingredients and baking method are called biscuits. The Scottish call the end product a scone.) Almost every baker in the state of Washington attempts to accomplish this piquant delicacy initiated by the Fischer Flour Company. I am no exception.

OVEN TIME: 5 minutes at 400 degrees
           15 minutes at 375 degrees

YIELD: 10 scones, or
        12 biscuits

3 cups unbleached white flour	¼ cup powdered sugar
⅔ teaspoons cream of tartar	⅔ cup butter
3½ teaspoons baking powder	¼ teaspoon vanilla
½ teaspoon sea salt	1 cup whole milk
2 Tablespoons full fat soy flour	

In large bowl, blend all dry ingredients together. With pastry blender or two knives, cut in butter until the mixture looks like a coarse grain. Add the milk and vanilla. Blend briskly with a fork. Squeeze the dough into a ball.

Turn out onto a floured board and pat into a ½ inch thick circular shape. Cut circle into pie-shaped wedges. Bake. Serve while piping hot with jam and butter.

WHEAT-FREE FLOUR SUBSTITUTES

1 cup of the following mix can be substituted for each cup of white flour in a recipe:

1 scant cup High-Lysine cornmeal or corn flour	⅞ cup brown rice flour
¾ cup soy flour	¾ cup oat flour
¾-⅞ cup barley flour	½ cup cornstarch
1 cup spelt flour	1½ cups rolled oats

1 cup kamut = 1 cup white flour.

All of the above can be blended together and stored. When making muffins or muffin mix, stir and measure from the container. Other flours, such as arrowroot, cornstarch, barley, potato flour, buckwheat, teff and amaranth can be added using ½ cup each. Pinto bean flour, navy bean, lima bean, etc. are good protein flours that can be utilized by adding one part to five parts wheat flour.

AMARANTH, POTATO AND QUINOA MUFFINS

OVEN TIME : 20 minutes at 400 degrees   **YIELD:** 9-10 muffins

2 eggs, separated	¼ teaspoon sea salt
¼ cup potato flour	2 Tablespoons sugar
2 Tablespoons amaranth flour	2 Tablespoons cold water
1½ Tablespoons quinoa flour	1 teaspoon soy milk powder
2 teaspoons baking powder	

Grease muffin tins and set aside. Blend together the potato flour, amaranth, quinoa flour and sea salt. In a large bowl, blend the egg yolks, water, 3 Tablespoons sugar and soy powder. In a separate bowl, beat the egg whites with 1 Tablespoon sugar to stiff moist peaks. Add the dry ingredients to the egg yolk mixture; gently fold in the whites. Bake. When the muffins are finished, turn out on a cooling rack.

"Agreeing with your adversary means only that it is right for him/her."
Edna Lister

BASIC WHEAT-FREE MUFFINS

OVEN TIME: 20 minutes at 400 degrees   **YIELD:** 12 muffins

    2 cups Wheat-Free   1 egg
       Muffin mix   1 cup milk, water, fruit
    ⅓ cup blended oil   puree, or fruit juice

Measure the dry ingredients and set aside. Measure the liquids into the mixing bowl and add the egg. Beat. Stir in the muffin mix. Mix only long enough to blend the ingredients. Spoon into oiled or sprayed muffin cups. Bake. When the muffins are finished, turn out on a cooling rack.

BRAN MUFFINS

OVEN TIME: 20 minutes at 400 degrees   **YIELD:** 12 muffins

    1½ cups all-bran   2 Tablespoons
     1 cup oat bran   soy milk powder
    ½ cup rice polish or bran   1 cup dates, soaked
    1½ teaspoons baking powder   2 eggs
    ¼ cup spelt, or   2 Tablespoons blended oil
       kamut flour   1½ cups nut seed
    ½ teaspoon sea salt   milk, or fruit juice
                                       Nuts and raisins, optional

Soak the dates in the ½ cup nut seed milk, milk, or fruit juice. Blend the dry ingredients. Set aside. In a large bowl, beat the eggs, then add the oil and liquid. Stir in the soaked dates. Add the dry ingredients. Stir in ⅓ cup each of nuts and raisins, if desired. Spoon into oiled muffin cups. Bake. When the muffins are finished, remove them from the pan. Cool on a rack.

Note: Rice polish or rice bran is the outer husk of rice which is high in some of the B vitamins. ¼ cup coarsley ground oatmeal may be susbstituted for the all-bran.

KAMUT-FLAX SEED YEAST MUFFINS

OVEN TIME: 20-25 minutes at 400 degrees   **YIELD:** 12 muffins

¼ cup warm water	2 Tablespoons butter, melted
2 teaspoons Saf yeast	¾ teaspoon sea salt
3 Tablespoons honey	3 Tablespoons flax seed meal
1 cup warm milk	2 cups kamut flour
2 eggs, separated	1 cup spelt flour
2 teaspoons orange zest	½ cup walnuts, chopped

Dissolve the yeast in the warm water. In a large bowl or electric mixer bowl, add the dissolved yeast, warm milk, honey and egg yolks. Blend. Add the orange zest and melted butter. Beat in 2 cups of the kamut flour. Beat 2 minutes. Blend together the remaining dry ingredients. Add to the batter. Beat to blend. Fold in the beaten egg whites and walnuts. Let rise in the mixing bowl until nearly doubled in bulk. Stir down. Spoon into prepared muffin cups. Let rise 15-20 minutes, or until the batter slightly arches over the cups. Bake. When baked, remove from the pan. Cool on a rack.

PEANUT MUFFINS

OVEN TIME: 20 minutes at 400 degrees   YIELD: 12 muffins

2 cups + 2 Tablespoons Wheat-Free Muffin mix	1 egg
¼ cup blended oil	1 cup milk, water, fruit puree, or fruit juice
⅓ cup chopped peanuts	

Measure the dry ingredients and set aside. Measure the liquids into the mixing bowl and add the egg. Beat. Stir in the muffin mix. Mix only long enough to blend the ingredients. Spoon into oiled or sprayed muffin cups. Bake. When the muffins are finished, turn out on a cooling rack.

Tip: Create surprises in muffins for your guests.
Centers can contain ½ teaspoon preserves, jam, chocolate chips or a cube of cream cheese.

 Wheat-Free Muffins

WHEAT-FREE CARROT MUFFINS

OVEN TIME: 20 minutes at 400 degrees   **YIELD:** 12 muffins

¼ cup barley flour
¼ cup brown rice flour
½ cup oat flour
½ teaspoon sea salt
1 teaspoon baking powder
½ teaspoon cinnamon
3 Tablespoons raisins

2 eggs, separated
3 Tablespoons blended oil
2 Tablespoons brown sugar
½ cup pineapple juice
1 cup carrots, grated
3 Tablespoons pecans, chopped

In a small bowl, blend the dry ingredients together. In a large mixing bowl, beat the liquid, egg yolks, sugar, oil and pineapple juice together. Stir in the dry ingredients. Mix only long enough to blend. Fold in the beaten egg whites, raisins and pecans. Fill prepared muffin tins ⅔ full. Bake. When the muffins are finished, remove from the pan. Cool on a rack.

"When a demand is made, the answer is already no."
Edna Lister

WHEAT-FREE DATE-BUTTER MUFFINS

OVEN TIME: 20 minutes at 400 degrees   **YIELD:** 12 muffins

2 cups Wheat-Free Muffin Mix
⅓ cup date sugar
   or brown sugar
1 egg

⅓ cup nut butter: sesame, almond, or peanut butter
1 cup milk, or fruit juice
¼ cup dates, diced

Measure the Muffin Mix into a small bowl. Set aside. In a large mixing bowl, blend all the liquid ingredients together. Stir in the muffin mix. Mix only long enough to blend. Fold in the dates. Fill prepared muffin tins ⅔ full. Bake. When the muffins are finished, remove from the pan. Cool on a rack.

Tip: Topping for muffins can be simple and flavorful. Blend 3 Tablespoons date sugar, 1 Tablespoon butter and ¼ teaspoon sugar. Crumble over the batter before baking.

WHEAT-FREE MUFFIN MIX

6 cups Wheat Free flour
  substitute
1½ teaspoons baking soda
2 Tablespoons soy
  milk powder
2 Tablespoons flax seed, ground

2 Tablespoons baking powder
1 Tablespoon sea salt
1 teaspoon cinnamon, optional
1 teaspoon unbuffered
  vitamin C

Blend all ingredients. Seal and refrigerate.

WHEAT-FREE PRUNE MUFFINS

OVEN TIME: 20 minutes at 400 degrees   **YIELD:** 12 muffins

1¼ cups kamut flour
6 cooked prunes
¼ cup brown rice flour
¼ teaspoon sea salt
1 teaspoon baking powder
$1/8$ teaspoon
  vitamin C powder
1 cup water, milk, or
  nut seed milk

2 Tablespoons barley flour
3 Tablespoons butter, melted
1 egg
3 Tablespoons blended oil
2 Tablespoons walnuts,
  Chopped

Sweeten as desired

In a small bowl, blend the dry ingredients together. In a large mixing bowl, beat the liquid, egg and butter together. Stir in the dry ingredients. Mix only long enough to blend. Fold in the prunes and walnuts. Fill prepared muffin tins ⅔ full. Bake. When the muffins are finished, remove from the pan. Cool on a rack.

Note: Frost with a mixture of cooked prunes and cream cheese, if desired.

Tip: Prunes may be a bit too acidic for some people, however they contain what some researchers call nerve salts. They contain high amounts of potassium and other valuable minerals. The high sugar content of dried prunes is easily assimilated by the body.

For crustier corn sticks, bake them in a pre-heated heavy skillet.

QUICK BREADS

The term "quick bread" includes tea loaves that are leavened with baking powder or baking soda. The advantage to quick breads is that the baking process is relatively speedy and straightforward. There are also drawbacks to the use of these leavening agents.

Prominent nutritionists have warned against the use of baking soda in foods, since it destroys the B-Complex vitamins. Baking powder also contains some of the same alkaline substance as baking soda. It is best to use baking powder and a small amount of baking soda together when sour milk, buttermilk, and other fermented dairy products are used in a recipe.

I sometimes add one or two calcium/magnesium tablets to the dough to bring about the "hook-up" of the natural phytic acid in the cereal grains so that it will not harm the calcium already present in the body. The addition of dairy products or another protein will neutralize some of the harmful effects of baking soda and baking powder also.

It might be fun to experiment with alternative leavening agents as well. Although it is more expensive, Potassium Bicarbonate may be used in a recipe in place of baking soda. Use it in the same amount as called for in the recipe. The product is available at pharmacies.

BATTER BREAD KNOW HOW

Batter bread differs from quick bread in that the leavening agent is yeast instead of baking powder or soda. The batter has to be beaten to perfection. Since double or triple rising time is not utilized, the gluten that supports the rising power has to be sufficiently developed.

It is the kneading process that develops the elasticity of the dough. Batter bread is allowed to rise in the mixing bowl. It is then stirred down and spooned into the baking pan. The batter is thick and tacky, so it needs to be pushed well into the corners of the pan.

The batter is allowed to rise once more in the baking pan, until it arches slightly over the top the pan before being placed in the oven. When the bread is baked, the crust will be thick, extra brown and craggy in appearance.

For best results, bake the loaf in a medium sized pan.

Quick Breads (117)

ALMOND TEA BREAD

OVEN TIME: 1 hour at 350 degrees

YIELD: 1 loaf

1 cup all-purpose flour
1 cup whole wheat pastry flour
½ teaspoon sea salt
½ teaspoon baking soda
2 teaspoons baking powder

1 large egg
⅔ cup brown sugar
¼ cup butter, melted
½ cup orange juice
½ cup milk
⅔ cup almonds, chopped
1 teaspoon almond flavoring

Preheat the oven. Spray the baking pan with vegetable spray. In a large bowl, combine all the dry ingredients, except the almonds and sugar. Set aside. In an electric mixer bowl, beat the egg, brown sugar and butter. Add the orange juice, flavoring and milk. Blend. Stir in the dry ingredients. Mix only long enough to blend the ingredients. Stir in the almonds.

Spoon the batter into the pan. Bake on the middle rack of the oven. Test for doneness by inserting a toothpick into the center. If it comes out clean, the loaf is finished.

Tip: Make Quick Breads more appealing by contrast in layering. Divide the dough in half. Add ¼ to the prepared pan. Reserve the remaining half, add ½ cube of semi-sweet chocolate, coconut or candied fruit and cream cheese. Spoon over the first ¼ of the mix. Top with the remaining ¼ of the batter. Bake.

APRICOT BUNDT CORNBREAD

Note: This cornbread is so fine-grained and flavorful dinner guests think that it's a cake. The bread is delightful when served with a Lincoln-style butter.

OVEN TIME: 55-60 minutes at 375 degrees   **YIELD:** 1 large bundt

1½ cups boiling water	1 cup buttermilk
1¾ cups High-Lysine cornmeal	¾ teaspoon baking soda
¼ cup butter	1½ teaspoon baking powder
½ teaspoon sea salt	1 Tablespoon soy flour
1 cup dried apricots, snipped	1 cup all-purpose flour
⅓ cup sugar	1 teaspoon sugar
4 eggs, separated	3 Tablespoons cornmeal (to dust the pan)

Add the boiling water to the cornmeal. Blend to remove lumps. Stir in the butter, sea salt and apricots. Set aside. In a large bowl, or an electric mixer bowl, beat the egg yolks and sugar together. Add the buttermilk and cornmeal mixture. In a separate bowl, blend together the baking soda, baking powder, soy flour and the all-purpose flour. Beat the egg whites with 1 teaspoon sugar until stiff, but not dry.

Add the dry ingredients. Stir only long enough to blend. Fold the egg whites into the batter. Turn the batter into a well-buttered tube pan which has been dusted with cornmeal. Bake. Let cool 5-6 minutes in the pan. Cool on a rack.

Tip: High Lysine cornmeal is finely ground. When substituting undergerminated cornmeal, remove 2 Tablespoons per cup and add 2 Tablespoons of flour.

Apricots and High-Lysine cornmeal are good food sources for this ESSENTIAL amino acid.

Apricot nectar would make a perfect liquid to use for one-half of the water called for in this recipe.

"Eternity is the period of time it takes to live an intense situation."
Linda Mahalic

BANANA NUT BREAD

Note: Quick breads have always been popular for ladies' teas, brunches and garden parties. Bananas, berries and other fresh fruits have always shared the limelight when they are presented for a classy affair.

OVEN TIME: 55 minutes at 350 degrees   **YIELD:** 1 loaf

1¼ cups unbleached white flour	¾ teaspoon sea salt
½ cup whole wheat pastry flour	¼ cup butter, melted
2 Tablespoons oatmeal	2 eggs
1 teaspoon baking powder	½ cup brown sugar
½ teaspoon baking soda	⅓ cup buttermilk
1 teaspoon vanilla, optional	2 large bananas, (approx. 1 cup)
	½ cup walnuts, chopped

Preheat the oven. Oil the baking pan. Blend together all the dry ingredients, except the brown sugar and the walnuts. Set aside. In an electric mixer bowl, beat the eggs, brown sugar and butter. Add the buttermilk. Stir in the dry ingredients. Mix only long enough to blend. Fold in the mashed bananas and the chopped walnuts. Spoon into the prepared pan. Let rest 3-5 minutes before placing in the oven. Bake on the middle rack. Let cool 5-6 minutes in the pan. Turn out onto a rack.

Tip: For people who are blessed with stomach trouble, remove the dark veins of seeds from the middle of the banana before eating. (They are very sharp).

"The measure of a person's character is not whether or not he/she fell, the issue is, did he/she get up and win the race".
Carter's Country Philosophy

CRACKLIN' CORN SPOON BREAD

Note: Because we were such a large family, and because it was hard times, some days our meals consisted of only corn products. We ate corn spoon bread with sorghum for breakfast and polenta for the evening meal. This recipe is typical of those days.

OVEN TIME: 20 minutes at 375 degrees **YIELD:** 1 loaf

2 eggs	½ teaspoon sea salt
3 Tablespoons sugar	½ teaspoon baking powder
¼ cup cream corn	¼ teaspoon baking soda
2 Tablespoons onion, minced	1 cup High-Lysine corn meal
½ cup pork cracklins	1-1⅓ cups unbleached white flour
1 cup buttermilk	

In a medium bowl, blend all the dry ingredients. Set aside. Heat a large cast iron skillet for 6-8 minutes. In an electric mixer bowl, beat together the eggs, sugar, corn, onion, cracklins and buttermilk. Add the dry ingredients. Stir only long enough to blend. Oil the hot skillet with olive oil spray. Pour the corn mixture into the pan. Bake. Serve hot with a honey butter mixture.

Note: In Rural America during the Great Depression, almost everything that we ate was prepared in our own kitchen. The pork "cracklins" in this bread recipe were cooked in the wood stove oven on butchering day. The pork skin, with the fat intact, was cubed and placed in a large pan. It was baked until all the fat was rendered. it was then strained through bleached flour sack material. The fat was removed from the heavy skin and ground, or diced.

CRANBERRY QUICK BREAD

Note: This Cranberry bread makes a lovely gift for the holidays. Bake it in a deep fluted pan and tuck it into a decorated basket with Cranberry butter or spread.

OVEN TIME: 55 minutes at 350 degrees   **YIELD:** 1 large bundt, or 2 loaves

3 large eggs	2 cups whole wheat pastry flour
¾ cup sugar	2½ teaspoons baking powder
⅓ cup butter	1 teaspoon baking soda
¾ teaspooon sea salt	1 cup unbleached white flour
1¼ cup plain yogurt	1 teaspoon sugar
1 Tablespoon orange zest	1 cup chopped cranberries
¼ cup soy flour	¾ cup chopped walnuts

Heat the oven. Spray the baking pan. In an electric mixer bowl, cream together 1 egg and 2 egg yolks, sugar, butter or margarine and sea salt. Stir in the yogurt and orange zest. In a separate bowl, blend together all the remaining dry ingredients, except the nuts. Beat the egg whites with the teaspoon sugar into soft moist peaks. (The addition of sugar will help the egg whites blend into the batter more readily.) Set aside.

Stir the dry ingredients into the yogurt mixture. Add the cranberries. Stir lightly. Fold in the egg whites and walnuts. Spoon into the baking pan. Bake. Test for doneness by inserting a toothpick into the center of the bread. It will come out clean when the bread is done. When the loaf is finished, let it rest in the pan for 5 minutes before removing it to a rack.

Note: When adding whole wheat flour the cranberries are not as prominent; however, the wheat flour adds nutrients to the recipe.

Tip: Soak 1 cup dried cranberries in ½ cup water for 1 hour or more. Use both liquid and whole berries.

DATE BREAD WITH FILLING

Note: This unique bread can be made with dates, prunes, apricots, or any dried fruit of your choice. Black wlanut bread with dried apples is particularly delicious. Feel free to experiment with different combinations.

OVEN TIME: 50-55 minutes at 350 degrees   **YIELD:** 1 loaf

7/8 cup whole wheat pastry flour	1/4 cup sour cream
1 cup unbleached white flour	1 cup buttermilk
2 Tablespoons soy milk powder	3/4 cup pecans, chopped
1/2 teaspoon baking soda	1 teaspoon vanilla, (optional)
1 teaspoon baking powder	FILLING
1/2 teaspoon sea salt	1 egg
2 eggs	6 ounces cream cheese, softened
2/3 cup brown sugar or date sugar	2 Tablespoons date sugar or brown sugar
3/4 cup dates, snipped	1 Tablespoon flour, or quick oats
1/4 cup butter, softened	

Blend all the dry ingredients together. Set aside. For Filling: in a seperate bowl, beat the egg or 2 egg whites, cream cheese, flour or quick oats and brown sugar, or date sugar. Set aside. In a large bowl or electric mixer beat together the eggs, brown sugar, butter, sour cream and vanilla. Add the buttermilk; stir to blend. Add the pecans and the dry ingredients. Stir only enough to blend. Spoon one-half of the mixture into the greased loaf pan.

Drop the filling by Tablespoons over the batter. Spoon the remainder of the batter on top of the filling. Place in a preheated oven and bake. Insert a toothpick into the center of the loaf; If the toothpick comes out clean, the loaf is done.

Note: Contrary to what we have always been taught, if we let the quick bread rest 5-8 minutes before placing it in the oven, the mixture will rise before the outside of the pan gets hot. When placing the bread in the oven, invert a loaf pan over the top of the bread pan. Remove it after 20 minutes of baking. This will help prevent deep cracks in the top of the loaf.

DATE NUT RING

The date sugar in the party Date Ring brings about a marriage of flavors that guests will love. It makes an excellent holiday party bread. The loaf can be decorated with stuffed dates surrounding the ring, and be served with a Date Cream Cheese filling.

OVEN TIME: 75 minutes at 350 degrees   **YIELD:** 1 Ring

1½ cups dates chopped	3 eggs
½ cup boiling water	2 cups unbleached white flour
1 cup date sugar, or brown sugar	¾ cup whole wheat flour
1 Tablespoon orange zest	2 teaspoons baking powder
1 cup milk	½ teaspoon sea salt
¼ cup butter, melted	1 teaspoon vanilla
	¾ cup pecans, chopped

Prepare the dates. Add the boiling water. (If desired, dates may be soaked in Madeira or fruit juice.) Set aside. Combine all of the dry ingredients. Stir. Set aside. Separate the eggs. Reserve the whites.

In a large bowl or electric mixer bowl, beat together the egg yolks, butter, and date sugar. Add the orange zest, milk, dates and flavoring. (Before adding the dry ingredients, beat the egg whites.)

In a separate bowl beat the egg whites until stiff, but not dry. (Adding 1 teaspoon sugar to the whites will help them to blend into the batter.) Add the dry ingredients to the batter. Blend, but do not overmix. Stir a small amount of the batter into the egg whites. Gently fold in the egg whites and the pecans. Spoon the batter into the prepared tube pan. Bake. Test with a toothpick for doneness. When the toothpick comes out clean, it is done. Let the loaf remain in the pan for 3-5 minutes before removing it to a cooking rack.

"Coming together is a beginning, keeping together is progress, working together is success."
Edna Lister

HIGH-FIBER BRAN BREAD

OVEN TIME: 40-45 minutes at 375 Degrees   **YIELD:** 2 loaves

2 eggs	1 cup bran
⅓ cup sugar	3 cups whole wheat flour
¼ cup butter	2 cups sour milk,
1 teaspoon baking soda	or buttermilk
1 teaspoon baking powder	1 cup prunes, chopped
1 teaspoon sea salt	¾ cup walnuts, chopped

In the mixer bowl, cream the eggs, butter and sugar. In a separate bowl, blend all dry ingredients, except the prunes and walnuts. Add the dry ingredients with the sour milk, alternating each addition. Do not over beat. Stir in the prunes and walnuts. Pour into greased bread pans. Bake. Cool on a rack. This batter will make lovely muffins also.

Tip: Fibrous residue in the daily diet is almost as important as drinking sufficient amounts of water.

Cereal grains will furnish some of the needed fiber. It is good to remember that fresh raw vegetables should be consumed at the same sitting in order that enzymatic performances can work synergistically with cooked foods, particularly when concentrated carbohydrate foods are eaten.

"There are 24 hours in a day, but make an effort to squeeze in that extra hour . . . it will pay dividends."
Edward Pembroke

PUMPKIN TEA BREAD

Note: The fall season here in the Northwest is a busy and exciting time. We gardeners are busy harvesting and preserving foodstuffs for the next year. If your only experience with pumpkin has been limited to the holiday meal, you're in for a surprise. This top-crop vegetable is very versatile. It can be used as a casserole dish, as a custard, as an addition to cheesecakes, or in a simple pie. This recipe was used in one portion of the "Creative Bread" demonstration at the Western Washington Fair.

OVEN TIME: 55-60 minutes at 350 degrees   **YIELD:** 1 large loaf

1½ cups unbleached white flour	½ teaspoon nutmeg
½ cup whole wheat flour	1 cup brown sugar
¾ teaspoon baking powder	⅓ cup butter or margarine
½ teaspoon baking soda	2 large eggs
½ teaspoon sea salt	¼ cup milk or light cream
¼ teaspoon ground cloves	1 cup pumpkin, pureed
1 teaspoon cinnamon	½ cup walnuts, chopped

Spray a standard-size loaf pan with olive oil spray. Dust with flour or cornmeal. Preheat the oven. In a medium bowl, blend together all the dry ingredients, except the walnuts. Set aside. In a large bowl or electric mixer bowl, beat together the brown sugar, butter, eggs, pumpkin puree and milk. Add the dry ingredients. Stir only long enough to blend the dry ingredients.

Fold in the walnuts. Turn the batter into the prepared pan. Push the batter well into the corners of the pan. Let the loaf rise for 3-5 minutes. Invert an empty loaf pan over the pumpkin pan. (This will prevent large cracking of the loaf during baking.) Bake 20 minutes. Carefully lift the pan from the baking bread. Continue the baking process. Test for doneness by inserting a toothpick into the top of the loaf. When the loaf is cooked, the toothpick will come out clean.

TOPPINGS FOR TEA BREADS. This topping is added before the bread is baked.

1½ Tablespoons butter	1 Tablespoon chopped pumpkin seeds
3 Tablespoons chopped walnuts	¼ teaspoon ground nutmeg
4 Tablespoons shredded coconut	2 Tablespoons brown sugar

Mix all the ingredients. Crumble evenly over the top of the loaf. Bake.

MUFFINS

MUFFIN SUCCESS

By all appearances, America has been visited by the muffin man! There are magnificent displays of muffins at every eatery, restaurant, coffee shop, and bed-and-breakfast. However, nutritionists determined long ago that foods prepared with acid-alkali leavening agents (e.g. baking powder and baking soda) will destroy vitamin B-1 (thiamin) in the recipe. Here are ten rules for successful muffin baking.

1. Greater success can be expected from quick batters when dairy products are added to the mixture. This is because protein will neutralize excess acids in recipes which call for baking powder and baking soda.

2. Purchase Low-Sodium baking powder at health food stores, kitchen shops, and stores where bulk grains and grinders are sold.

3. Once the muffin mixing procedure begins, proceed quickly without stopping. Mix the wet and dry ingredients only long enough to combine them.

4. Even though it is wise to cut down on fat in the diet, baked goods need some oil for several reasons, namely:
Fat improves the texture and tenderness of the product;
Fat imparts flavor and richness to the product;
Fat molecules coat the gluten to give the product, flaky light interior.
Lecithin is made from defatted soybeans. It will also split and disperse the fat molecules throughout the structure of the product.

5. Adding beaten egg whites to sticky, chopped or candied fruits before folding them into the batter will make them blend more easily.

6. Add 1 teaspoon sugar to the egg whites while beating and then add a small amount of the batter to the whites before blending them into the main batter. The batter will then accept the whites quickly and evenly.

7. Muffin cup liner papers may save washing pans, but they will pull away part of the muffin, or cup cake.

8. Because muffins contain eggs, milk, meats, etc., they must be refrigerated or frozen until needed.

9. Olive oil vegetable coating spray is one simple way of preparing muffin cups for baking.

10. Different flour and brands of flour react differently in liquids. It is wise to make a quick test before baking with a different brand or type of flour.

Note: All the muffins in this book can be made using either the Wholesome Muffin Mix or the Basic Muffin Mix. Use 2-2¼ cups mix to 1 cup liquid. 1 egg = ¼ cup liquid.

APPLE NUT MUFFINS

OVEN TIME: 20 minutes at 400 degrees   **YIELD:** 12 muffins

2 cups Wholesome Muffin Mix	½ teaspoon cinnamon
2 medium eggs	3 Tablespoons canola oil
⅓ cup apple, diced	⅓ cup walnuts, chopped
1 cup milk	2 Tablespoons sugar, optional

Beat the eggs. Add the oil and milk. Add the muffin mix and cinnamon. Beat only enough to combine the ingredients. Fold in the apple and walnuts. Spoon into prepared pans. Bake. When muffins are finished, remove from the pan. Cool on a rack.

Note: These muffins brown quickly due to the addition of soy products and whey powder. They also have a snappy crust.

Tip: When Cottage Cheese is used in a recipe, it is best to drain the cheese before it is pureed. Rinsing the cheese lightly in a colander will remove some of the additive materials used during processing. Puree with sour cream or the egg to be used in the recipe. High cooking temperatures destroy vitiman A.

BLUEBERRY CHEESE-YOGURT DOUBLE-MUFFINS

Note: The addition of yogurt cream cheese creates a finely textured, healthy muffin.

OVEN TIME: 25 minutes at 400 degrees

YIELD: 12 double-size muffins

⅔ cup cottage cheese, pureed	¾ teaspoon sea salt
2 teaspoons orange concentrate	3 teaspoons baking powder
¼ cup milk	1 teaspoon baking soda
2 eggs	1 cup blueberries, blotted
⅔ cup sugar	⅓ cup slivered almonds
2 Tablespoons Blended oil	2 cups all-purpose flour
¼ cup quick oats	4 6 ounces cubes cream cheese

Spray the muffin cups with vegetable spray. Set aside. Preheat the oven. Puree the cottage cheese and orange concentrate. Blend all the dry ingredients together. Set aside. In a large bowl or electric mixer bowl, beat the eggs, oil, and sugar together. Add the cheese puree.

Blend in the dry ingredients. Stir only long enough to combine. Carefully fold in the blueberries. Place the batter in the muffin cups, using a ¼ cup measure. Place 1'' square of cream cheese in the center. Add ¼ cup more batter. (You can also garnish the top with more cheese.) Bake on the middle shelf of the oven. When baked, remove the muffins from the pan. Cool on a rack.

Note: These muffins are also rich enough to serve as a dessert. Simply split the muffins in half, crosswise. Place the halves in individual deep-dishes and top with a mixture of semi-sweetened cooked blueberry sauce and fresh uncooked pineapple chunks. Top with whipped cream and a scattering of fresh blueberries and slivered almonds.

CARROT-ORANGE BRAN MUFFINS

OVEN TIME: 20 minutes at 400 degrees   **YIELD:** 12 muffins

¾ cup all-purpose flour	1 egg
¾ cup whole wheat flour	3 Tablespoons butter
1 cup all bran, or Miller's bran	3 Tablespoons frozen orange concentrate
3 teaspoons baking powder	¼ cup honey
½ teaspoon baking soda	1 cup carrot, grated
½ teaspoon sea salt	1 cup milk
½ teaspoon cinnamon	½ cup pecans, chopped

Heat the oven. Spray the muffin pans. In a large bowl, combine the all-purpose flour, whole wheat flour, all bran, or Miller's bran, baking powder, baking soda, sea salt and cinnamon. Set aside.

In an electric mixer bowl, beat together the eggs, butter, orange concentrate and honey. Stir in the milk and grated carrot. Add the dry mixture. Stir only long enough to blend the ingredients. Fold in the pecans. Spoon into muffin cups. Fill ⅔ full. Bake. When finished, remove from the pan. Cool on a rack.

Tip: Minerals in their most soluble form can be extracted from vegetable cellulose. Carrots are but one of the vegetables that blend well with oranges and cereal grains. Carrot juice may be used for a portion of the liquid in this recipe, however, its electrical impulses, gleaned from the sun's rays may be lost or diminished.

"Do not waste precious moments crying about things that are withheld from us. Simple praise and joy going forth will attract God's own for us, and to us at once."
Edna Lister

CARROT-RAISIN STICKY MUFFINS

Note: These muffins have a soft, light texture and color. Their semi-sweet body is coated with a maple-flavored crunchy glaze. These muffins are excellent to serve for brunches for afternoon tea. They also make a lovely holiday gift.

OVEN TIME: 20 minutes at 400 degrees   **YIELD:** 12-14 muffins

1½ cups whole wheat flour	¾ teaspoon sea salt
½ cup oatmeal, or Pantry Enrichment Mix	1 cup buttermilk
¾ teaspoon pumpkin pie spice	3 Tablespoons canola oil
	⅓ cup brown sugar
	2 eggs
1 teaspoon baking powder	½ cup raisins, chopped
1 teaspoon baking soda	½ cup walnuts, chopped

Spray the muffin cups with a vegetable coating spray. Spoon the glaze into the muffin cups. Blend all the dry ingredients, except the raisins, nuts and brown sugar. Set aside. Beat together eggs, canola oil, brown sugar and buttermilk. Add the dry ingredients. Blend. Mix only long enough to combine the ingredients. Stir in the raisins and walnuts. Spoon batter carefully into the glaze. Fill each cup ½-⅔ full. Bake. Place a baking pan or wax paper under the cooling rack to catch the excess glaze. Remove the muffins from the oven and invert the muffins on the rack.

GLAZE:

2 Tablespoons butter	⅓ cup brown sugar, firmly packed
½ medium apple, diced	
2 Tablespoons water	⅓ cup walnuts, finely chopped

Melt the butter, add the brown sugar and water. Stir until the sugar dissolves. Add the apple and walnuts. Spoon evenly into the muffin cups.

"Watching television is watching others develop their talents when we should be developing our own."
Ferne Chapman

CARTER'S COUNTRY BRAN MUFFINS

Note: Our country muffins were made in makeshift pans. The pans included every type of container that would hold the batter: jar lids, tin cans, hotel or railroad stoneware mugs, etc. No matter how we baked them, the muffins were simply delicious.

OVEN TIME: 20 minutes at 400 degrees   **YIELD:** 12 muffins

1 cup unbleached white flour	2 eggs
½ cup whole wheat flour	½ cup brown sugar
4 teaspoons baking powder	3 Tablespoons butter
1¼ cups Miller's bran	¼ cup molasses
2 Tablespoons oatmeal	1 cup milk
½ teaspoon sea salt	¼ cup apple juice
	½ cup walnuts

Spray the muffin tins with olive oil spray and set aside. Heat the oven. Combine the white flour, whole wheat flour, baking powder, Miller's bran, oatmeal, and sea salt. Set aside.

In an electric mixer bowl, beat together the eggs, brown sugar, butter and molasses. Beat well. Add the milk and apple juice. Blend. Add the flour mixture. Stir only long enough to blend. Add the walnuts. Spoon the batter into the muffin cups. Fill ⅔ full. Bake. Remove the muffins from the pan. Cool on a rack.

Note: Country folks stored grains in the outdoor granary. My mother Lillian would stand on the north porch, pouring grain berries from pan to pan, letting the brisk wind sift the chaff and debris away. The grains were washed, soaked and cooked for cereal, breads and casserole baking.

 Muffins

CHUNKY APPLE-CARROT MUFFINS WITH OAT BRAN

Note: The compatibility of these fruits and vegetables makes a deliciously nutritious accompaniment to any breakfast, brunch or afternoon tea.

OVEN TIME: 20 minutes at 375 degrees   **YIELD:** 16 muffins

1½ cups unbleached white flour	2 eggs
1 cup whole wheat pastry flour	⅔ cup brown sugar
¼ cup oat bran	1 raw carrot, grated
2 Tablespoons soy milk pwder	3 Tablespoons blended oil
½ teaspoon nutmeg	1 cup chunky apple sauce
¼ teaspoon allspice	1 cup buttermilk
½ teaspoon sea salt	¾ raw apple, diced
3 teaspoons baking powder	½ cup choppped walnuts

Spray the muffin pans with an olive oil spray. Stir together all the dry ingredients. Set aside. In a large bowl or electric mixer bowl, beat the eggs, brown sugar and oil. Stir in the raw carrots, apple sauce and buttermilk. Slowly stir in dry ingredients. Do not overmix.

Stir in the raw apple and walnuts. Spoon mixture into the muffin cups. Fill ½-⅔ full. Bake. When baked, remove the muffins from the pan immediately. On cooling rack, turn bottom side up to expose the glaze.

Note: If desired, these muffins may be dipped in melted butter and cinnamon sugar after baking.

"A spicy spirit and praise of God always wins the battle."
Edna Lister

CRANBERRY CREAM CHEESE MUFFINS

Note: It's economical to purchase a large amount of cranberries during the holiday season. Cranberries freeze well and can be dried easily in a home fruit dryer.

OVEN TIME: 20 minutes at 375 degrees   **YIELD:** 12 muffins

1¼ cups plus 2 Tablespoons unbleached white flour	1 Tablespoon lemon juice
2 teaspoons baking powder	3 Tablespoons sesame seed oil
½ teaspoon baking soda	¼ cup honey
2 Tablespoons soy milk powder or Enrichment Mix	¾ cup milk
	8 ounces cream cheese
½ teaspoon sea salt	½ cup dried cranberries
2 eggs, separated	½ cup walnuts, chopped

Spray the muffin tins with olive oil spray. Set aside. Combine all of the dry ingredients. Stir. Set aside. Separate the eggs. Reserve the whites. Cut the cream cheese in half. Cut the half into 12 cubes. Set aside.

In a large bowl or electric mixer bowl, beat together the egg yolks, sesame seed oil, honey, milk, 4 ounces of the cream cheese and lemon juice. In a separate bowl beat the egg whites until stiff, but not dry. (Adding 1 teaspoon sugar to the whites will help them to blend into the batter.)

Add the dry ingredients to the batter. Blend, but do not overmix. Stir in the dried cranberries and walnuts. Gently fold in the egg whites. Spoon the batter into the muffin cups. Fill ½-⅔ full. Sprinkle with a few walnut bits. Press the cream cheese cubes into the center of each muffin. Bake. Remove the muffins from the pan. Cool on a rack.

NOTE: Cranberry spread is delicious with these muffins. Soften 3 ounces of cream cheese and add 2 Tablespoons of whole cranberry sauce. Blend together. Refrigerate until needed.

"Compassion is the desire to assist."
Linda Mahalic

DATE AND OAT MUFFINS

Note: Oats are another example of a food substance that was formerly used almost exclusively for animal nutrition. It is now considered to be one of the superfoods, and an excellent source of fiber in the diet. Natural oat berries, cooked, or sprouted, oat flakes, quick oatmeal, and oat bran can be used in many different dishes.

OVEN TIME: 20 minutes at 400 degrees   **YIELD:** 12 muffins

½ cup low-fat yogurt
⅔ cup milk
2 Tablespoons
   soy milk powder
½ cup quick oats
⅓ cup snipped dates
⅓ teaspoon allspice
3 Tablespoons blended oil
2 eggs
⅓ cup brown sugar

2 teaspoons sea salt
1½ cups unbleached
   white flour
2 teaspoons baking powder
½ teaspoon baking soda
½ cup walnuts, chopped
GLAZE:
¼ cup brown sugar
4 Tablespoons orange juice
3 Tablespoons butter
2 Tablespoons water

In a large bowl, blend together the yogurt, milk, soy milk powder, quick oats and dates. Set aside for 10 minutes. Spray the muffin cups. Combine ingredients for the glaze. Divide it equally between the cups.

Blend together the allspice, flour, sea salt, baking powder, and baking soda. Set aside. Beat the eggs, oil and sugar together. Add the mixture to the yogurt-oatmeal mixture. Stir in dry ingredients. Do not overmix. Spoon mixture over the brown sugar glaze. Fill the cups ⅔-¾ full. Bake. When the muffins are finished, remove them immediately from the pan. Invert them on a cooling rack to expose the glaze.

"Enthusiasm is the mother of effort, and without it nothing great is ever accomplished."
Edna Lister

FRUIT COCKTAIL MUFFINS

OVEN TIME: 25 minutes at 400 degrees

YIELD: 12 muffins
or 6 double muffins

2½ cups Basic Muffin mix	2 Tablespoons canola oil
1 teaspoon cinnamon	1 egg
¼ teaspoon ground cloves	⅓ cup brown sugar
¼ teaspoon nutmeg	½ cup plain yogurt
½ teaspoon baking soda	¾ cup fruit cocktail
½ cup cashews, chopped	¼ cup fruit cocktail liquid

Spray the muffin cups with olive oil spray. If muffin cup liners are used, spray the inside of the paper. Set aside. Combine the Muffin Mix, cinnamon, nutmeg, cloves, baking soda and cashews in a small bowl. Set aside.

In a large bowl or electric mixer bowl, beat together the eggs, brown sugar, canola oil, yogurt, and the fruit cocktail liquid. Add the milk. Add the dry mixture to the liquid. Blend only long enough to combine the ingredients. Stir in the fruit cocktail. Place ½ cup batter in each doubled muffin cup. Bake on the middle rack of the oven. When the muffins are finished, remove from the pan. Cool on a rack.

GOLDEN CORN MUFFINS

OVEN TIME: 20 minutes at 400 degrees

YIELD: 12 muffins

1 cup unbleached white flour	1 egg
¾ cup High-Lysine corn meal	¼ cup butter, melted
½ teaspoon sea salt	3 Tablespoons sugar or honey
2½ teaspoons baking powder	1 cup whole milk
3 Tablespoons quick oatmeal	½ cup cashews, or sunflower seeds

In a medium-size bowl, blend together all the dry ingredients. Set aside. In an electric mixer bowl, beat together the egg, butter and sugar. Add the milk. Stir in the dry ingredients. Stir only long enough to blend. Place in a prepared muffin tin. Bake. When the muffins are finished, remove them from the cups to a cooling rack.

JACK O' LANTERN MUFFINS

Note: Farm-fresh food products are not unique to country folks; they are readily available to everyone who takes the time to search them out. Halloween or Thanksgiving time is the prime time for purchasing pumpkins. Even the Jack O' Lantern can be salvaged. Wash the outside of the pumpkin with a mild solution of household bleach in water (1 Tablespoon to 1 gallon of water). Rinse well. Dry the pumpkin. Cut away all debris from the inside. Remove the skin and steam on top of the stove in a small amount of water, or bake it in the skin in a 325 degree oven until soft. Remove the meat from the skin. Store it in pre-measured amounts until needed.

OVEN TIME: 20 minutes at 375 degrees   **YIELD:** 12-14 muffins

1 cup whole wheat flour	2 eggs
1 cup unbleached white flour	½ cup sour cream
¼ teaspoon nutmeg	¼ cup orange juice concentrate
½ teaspoon cinnamon	
½ teaspoon sea salt	1 cup pumpkin puree
1¼ teaspoons baking soda	½ cup brown sugar
1 teaspoon baking powder	¼ cup milk
	3 Tablespoons pumpkin seeds, chopped

Spray the muffin tins with olive oil spray. Set aside. Combine all of the dry ingredients. Stir. Set aside.

In a large bowl or electric mixer bowl, beat together the eggs, sour cream, orange concentrate, pumpkin puree, brown sugar and milk. Add the dry ingredients to the batter. Blend, but do not overmix. Stir in 2 Tablespoons of the pumpkin seeds. Reserve the remainder of the seeds for the top. Spoon the batter into the muffin cups. Fill ½-⅔ full. Sprinkle the muffins with the remaining pumpkin seeds. Bake. Remove the muffins from the tin. Cool on a rack.

NOTE: A brown sugar glaze may be spooned into the bottom of each muffin cup, if desired. See Date Oat Muffin glaze.

OKTOBERFEST MUFFINS

Note: When it comes to making wise choices in food selections, try something new for Oktoberfest: fall-colored magnificent muffins. They please both the eye and the palate.

OVEN TIME: 20 minutes at 375 degrees   **YIELD:** 16 muffins

1 cup unbleached white flour	¼ cup butter
1¼ cups whole wheat flour	⅔ cup brown sugar
3 teaspoons baking powder	½ cup sweet potatoes, cooked, mashed
¾ teaspoon sea salt	½ cup pumpkin puree
1 teaspoon pumpkin pie spice	1 cup apricot juice
2 eggs, separated	½ cup pecans, chopped
1 teaspoon sugar	

Spray the muffin pans with a vegetable spray. Set aside. Stir together all the dry ingredients except the pecans. Set aside. In a large bowl or electric mixer bowl, beat the eggs, butter, brown sugar, sweet potatoes, pumpkin and apricot juice.

Stir in dry ingredients. Mix only enough to combine the ingredients. Stir in the roasted pecans. Spoon the mixture into the muffin cups. Fill ½-⅔ full. Bake. Remove muffins from the pan immediately. Cool on a rack.

Note: Both the apricots and pumpkin contain rich amounts of vitamin A, vitamin B complex, with the exception of biotin a vitamin E, both are rich in potassium and contain other minerals. They each contain small amounts of 18 amino acids, (proteins). Sweet potato is deficient in biotin, vitamin E and selenium. Excessive heat causes the destruction of vitamin A and many of the B vitamins. The minerals are more stable.

FAMILY FAVORITES

1926 - 1930 Something Recipes

CARROT FIBER SPELT BREAD

Note: Making carrot fiber spelt bread is one way to utilize the leftover carrot pulp from juicing. The bread is excellent when freshly sliced, dried in a low-temperature oven, or used as rusks with soup and salads. No matter how it's served, it's a treat.

OVEN TIME: 30 minutes at 400 degrees   **YIELD:** 2 large loaves

2 cups warm water	2 Tablespoons soy flour
2 Tablespoons instant dry yeast	1 cup carrot pulp, heated
2 Tablespoons honey	3 Tablespoons sunflower seeds
2 Tablespoons molasses	2 cups bread flour
3 Tablespoons sunflower seed oil	11-11½ cups spelt flour
½ cup plain yogurt	1 egg white
	2 Tablespoons water

In a large bowl, or in an electric mixer bowl, dissolve the yeast in warm water. Add the honey. Let rest until foamy, if time permits. Beat in the bread flour with 1 cup of spelt flour. Beat 2 minutes. Add the molasses. If time allows, turn the motor off and let the sponge rest until bubbly. Add the yogurt, sunflower seed oil, soy flour, carrot pulp, and sunflower seeds. Beat to blend.

Gradually add the remaining spelt flour. Beat after each addition. Scrape down the inside of the bowl. When the dough begins to leave the side of the bowl, turn it out onto a sprinkling of flour. Knead 6-8 minutes, or until the dough becomes smooth and elastic. If the carrot pulp has not been heated sufficiently, the live enzymes will make the dough tacky. Be patient and sprinkle a small amount of flour over the dough.

Place the dough in an oiled bowl. Turn to coat all sides with oil. Let rise until doubled in bulk. Punch down. Let rise again. Turn the dough out on a flat surface. Press out the air bubbles. Form dough into loaves. Place in loaf pans. Cover with a light cloth. Let rise until nearly doubled. Brush with the egg white mixture. Bake. When the bread is finished, remove it from the pans. Cool on a rack.

"Our net worth is what we are worth after deductions."
Edna Lister

CARROT RAISIN SALAD BRAID

Note: Innovative procedures in the kitchen will save you money, help recycle food, and furnish extra fiber for the diet. Think of leftovers, such as carrot-raisin salad, as a fortifier for the next batch of bread. Since the salad usually contains mayonnaise, nuts and raisins, it must be tightly covered and refrigerated until needed. Some vitamins are lost when food is held over; however, the minerals, amino acids and fiber are retained.

OVEN TIME: 35-40 minutes at 375 degrees   **YIELD:** 1 long braid

1 cup warm potato water	¼ cup butter, melted
4 teaspoons Saf yeast	2 Tablespoons soy milk powder
¼ cup sugar, or honey	1¼ teaspoons sea salt
1 cup light cream	250 milligrams vitamin C
2 eggs	1 teaspoon cinnamon
1¼ cups carrot salad	8½-9 cups unbleached white flour

In a large bowl or electric mixer bowl, dissolve the yeast in the warm potato water and add the sugar. Let the mixture rest until foamy. Add 1½ cups flour. Beat 2 minutes. Add the eggs, 1 at a time, beating the mixture after each addition. Stir in the cream, butter and carrot salad. Blend. Scrape down the inside of the bowl.

In a separate bowl, blend 3 cups of the remaining flour with the soy milk powder, sea salt, vitamin C and cinnamon. Gradually add it to the batter. When the dough leaves the side of the bowl, turn it out onto a sprinkling of flour. Knead until smooth and elastic. Make a ball of the dough and place it in an oiled bowl. Turn to coat all sides. Cover and let rise until doubled in bulk. Punch down. Turn out and press out the remaining air bubbles.

Divide the dough into ⅓-⅔ portions. Roll the larger piece into a rectangle, approximately 13-14 inches long. Cut it into 3 equal strips with a plastic pizza cutter. Braid the strips and pinch the ends to seal. Place the loaf on an oiled baking sheet. Repeat the process with the next portion of dough, rolling it 1½ inch shorter than the first portion of dough. Braid the strips. Seal the ends. Make a hollow in the center of the first braid. Brush the hollow with egg white. Lay the second braid in the groove. Tuck more walnuts and raisins into the braids if desired. Cover and let rise until nearly doubled in bulk. Brush with an egg white and water mixture. Bake.

COUNTRY GARDEN BREAD

Note: This Country Garden bread is especially good served piping hot for summertime patio parties. The bread can be made using two different methods. If time allows, let your guests pick and steam their own vegetable combination on the grill. Place the vegetables in small serving boats and cover with parchment paper, or another suitable lid. Have the bread dough prepared to use after the first rising. Let each individual roll and fold their own vegetables into their roll. Let rise, bake and serve. The second method is a hassle-free method. The following recipe releases you from cooking while guests are present.

OVEN TIME: 35 minutes at 375 degrees
20 minutes (rolls)

YIELD: 2 1½ pound loaves
4 large dinner rolls

2½ cups warm water	2 teaspoons sea salt
5 teaspoons instant dry yeast	1½ Tablespoons oil blend
2 Tablespoons honey	⅔ cup Swiss or Mozzerella cheese, grated
½ cup milk	2 Tablespoons soy milk powder
2 Tablespoons Country Garden Dried Vegetables, or vegetable seasoning	2 cups unbleached white flour
	6-6½ cups whole wheat flour

In a large mixing bowl or electric mixer bowl, dissolve the yeast in the warm water. Add the honey. If time permits, let rest for 10 minutes. Add the milk. Add 2 cups white flour. Beat 2 minutes.

Add the Country Vegetable Seasoning. Beat. Scrape the sides of the bowl. Add the sea salt, oil and cheese. Blend. Add 2 cups whole wheat flour. Beat 2 minutes. Gradually add the remaining flour and soy powder. When the dough begins to leave the sides of the bowl, turn the dough out onto a sprinkling of flour. Knead for 6-8 minutes, or until the dough is smooth and elastic. Place it in an oiled bowl, turn to coat all sides of the dough with oil. Cover. Let rise until doubled in bulk.

Turn the dough out onto a sprinkling of flour. Press out the air bubbles. Knead 5-6 minutes. Divide the dough. Form the loaves. Place in greased loaf pans. Let rise until doubled in bulk. Brush tops lightly with egg white and water mixture. Bake. When the loaves are finished, remove from the pan. Cool on a rack. (Bake dinner rolls 20 minutes.)

 Family Favorites

FRIED GREEN TOMATO BREAD

Note: The folks from the "Old Country" set the standard for fried green tomatoes. They were served as a side-dish at almost every meal during the fall harvest. Green tomato relish, green tomato jelly, and jars of canned ripe tomatoes lined root-cellar shelves. The remainder of the tomato harvest was wrapped (one tomato in each sheet of the funny papers) and stored under the bed until they ripened. It was time-consuming to unwrap each tomato, every other day, to check its ripeness. But in those days we had more time.

OVEN TIME: 35 minutes at 375 degrees   **YIELD:** 2 loaves

1 cup chicken broth	1 small onion, chopped
1 cup warm water	1 Tablespoon pizza seasoning
4 teaspoons instant dry yeast	2 Tablespoons soy oil
2 Tablespoons sugar or honey	3 Tablespoons wheat germ
2 Tablespoons gluten	2 teaspoons sea salt
1 teaspoon lecithin, optional	3 cups unbleached white flour
3 green tomatoes, diced	2-2½ cups whole wheat flour

In a small frying pan, saute the onion in 2 teaspoons olive oil until transparent. Remove it from the pan. Set aside. Remove blemishes from the tomato, dice and saute lightly. Remove the tomatoes from the pan with a slotted spoon. Drain. Cool to warm. Set aside.

In a large bowl or electric mixer bowl, dissolve the yeast in the warm water and chicken broth. Add the sugar or honey. Add the white flour. Beat 2 minutes. In a small bowl mix the gluten, lecithin, sea salt, pizza seasoning and wheat germ with 1 cup of whole wheat flour. Set aside. Add the oil. Gradually add the remaining flour. Beat after each addition. Scrape down the inside of the bowl. When the dough begins to climb the dough hook; turn it out on a flat surface onto a sprinkling of flour. Knead well. Flatten the dough with the palms. Add the fried green tomatoes and onions. Fold the dough several times to work in the vegetables. Place the dough in an oiled bowl. Turn to coat all sides of the dough. Cover. Let rise until doubled in bulk.

Punch the dough down. Turn out on a flat surface and press out the remaining air bubbles. Divide the dough and let rest for 3-4 minutes. Form the loaves. Place in sprayed pans. Cover and let rise until nearly doubled. Whisk 1 egg white with 2 Tablespoons of water and brush the top of the loaves. Diagonal slits may be cut in the top of the loaves, if desired. Stuff tomato and onion slices into the slits. Sprinkle with Parmesan Cheese. Bake. When the bread is finished, remove it from the pan.
Cool on a rack.

GREAT GRANDPA'S APPLE DUMPLINGS

Note: The Apple Dumplings rest in a sea of sweet liquid.

OVEN TIME: 55-60 minutes at 350 degrees   **YIELD:** 4 servings

½ cup water	¼ teaspoon cinnamon
½ cup sugar	1 teaspoon butter
4 apples	½ teaspoon salt
2 eggs	½ teaspoon vanilla flavoring
¼ cup water	1 teaspoon baking powder
1 cup sugar	1 cup flour
Nuts, chopped, optional	

In a medium saucepan, simmer the apples in water for 10 minutes. Beat the eggs and stir in the sugar and liquid ingredients. Beat in the remaining ingredients. Pour over the apples. Bake until brown.

GREEN TOMATO MINCEMEAT (1924)

Note: This North Dakota recipe was always requested at tomato harvest time.

Chop, drain, and scald, twice, one peck of green tomatoes (8 quarts); add 2 pounds of raisins chopped, 1 cup of suet, 2 Tablespoons salt, and 5 pounds white sugar; cook until tender, and when cool, add 1 cup of vinegar, 2 Tablespoonful each of cloves, cinnamon and allspice, 1 nutmeg (grated), and the juice of 2 lemons. Pack into sterilized jars and seal while hot.

"Take no offense at people, they do not know your soul
as The Master does."
God Calling, Daily Devotional

NETTIE HOWE'S BAGGS

DEEP FRYER

3 eggs	1 cup sugar
2 Tablespoons butter, melted	1 teaspoon vanilla
2 Tablespoons milk	2 cups all-purpose flour
½ teaspoon salt	Coating:
½ teaspoon cinnamon	1½ cups powdered sugar

Beat the eggs until light. Add butter, milk, sugar, salt and vanilla. Add the flour and beat. Divide the dough. Roll very thin. Tear off pieces with a fork. Lower each piece carefully into hot oil.

Drain on dry bread crusts, or on paper towels. Roll in the cinnamon sugar mixture.

"Your prayers are the conduit which link others to God."
Edna Lister

LILLIAN'S BASIC WHITE BREAD

THE ALL AMERICAN STANDBY

Note: People usually enjoy the taste of yeast and relate it to the nostalgic down-home aroma of baking bread. Our country kitchen was inundated with those great smells. Luscious yeasty scents meant home, security and love to us. It was right up there with mamma's apron (which we bashfully hid behind when company arrived), the first flame of the kindling wood (so we could start a meal), and the fragrance of baking bread when we came in from the fields, worn-to-a-frazzle. I wouldn't bet that Grandma would love baking bread in these "new fangled machines." Folks in those days had the idea that the more work a project took, the better the outcome. They were usually right. What she would love, I'm sure, is the easy availability of ingredients, real measuring paraphernalia and standardized bread pans.

OVEN TIME: 30 minutes at 400 degrees   **YIELD:** 2 loaves

½ cup mashed potato	¼ cup sour cream
2 cups milk, scalded	¼ cup sugar
5 teaspoons instant yeast	¼ teaspoon ground ginger
½ cup water	2 teaspoons salt
1 teaspoon sugar	2 eggs
3 Tablespoons butter, melted	8½-9 cups all-purpose flour

Heat the milk to simmer in a medium saucepan. Remove from the heat. Cool to just warm to the touch. In a large bowl or electric mixer bowl dissolve the yeast in the warm water. Add the teaspoon of sugar. Stir in the potato and milk. Add 3 cups flour. Beat 2 minutes. Scrape down the inside of the bowl. Add the butter, sour cream, remaining sugar and salt. Blend well. Add the eggs, one at a time. Beat after each egg. Scrape down the inside of the bowl.

Blend the ginger with the remaining flour. Gradually add it to the batter. When the dough leaves the side of the bowl, turn it out onto a sprinkling of flour. Knead until the dough is smooth and elastic. Place it in an oiled bowl. Turn to coat all sides with oil. Cover. Let rise until doubled in bulk. Punch down. Turn out on a flat surface. Press out the remaining air bubbles. Divide the dough into equal portions. Form the loaves and place in sprayed baking pans. Let rise until nearly doubled in bulk. Bake. When the loaves are finished, remove them from the pan. Cool on a rack.

 Family Favorites

POTATO SALAD BREAD

Note: This improvisational recipe allows you to use the leftover potato salad. The potato salad includes the usual: eggs, celery, sweet pickles, onions, mayonnaise and sour cream. When the potato salad is pureed only tiny speckles of the greens are visible. The resulting bread has an excellent texture and flavor. (Bake this bread immediately, since it is unsafe to carry-over the eggs and mayonnaise.)

OVEN TIME: 35-40 minutes at 400 degrees   **YIELD:** 2 loaves

1 cup water	1½ cups potato salad, pureed
1 Tablespoon Saf yeast	3 Tablespoons sesame seed oil
1 Tablespoon sugar	
¼ cup non-fat dry milk	1¼ teaspoons sea salt
	5-5½ cups bread flour

In a large bowl, or in an electric mixer bowl, dissolve the yeast in warm water. Add the sugar, nonfat dry milk and potato salad puree. Beat to blend. Add 2 cups flour. Beat 2 minutes. Turn off the motor. Scrape down the inside of the bowl. Add the sesame oil and sea salt. Gradually add the remaining flour. Beat after each addition. Scrape down the bowl at intervals. When the dough begins to climb the dough hook, turn it out on a flat surface in a sprinkling of flour. Knead until smooth and elastic. (This dough will be a bit tacky.) Place the dough in an oiled bowl. Turn to coat all sides with oil. Cover. Let rise until doubled in bulk.

Punch the dough down. Turn out on a flat surface and press out the remaining air bubbles. Divide the dough. Form the loaves. Place in oiled pans. Cover. Let rise until slightly above the top of the pan. Brush the top of the loaves with oil. Bake. When the loaves are finished, remove from the pans. Cool on a rack.

Some pioneers built their homes of native stone.

RICE PUDDING BREAD

Note: Due to a lack of refrigeration on the farm, food had to be recycled immediately. Granted, some of the food value is lost during reheating, but the fiber and carbohydrates were not wasted. This bread rises and browns beautifully. The flavor and texture will not suffer because of the seemingly strange addition.

OVEN TIME: 30-35 minutes at 400 degrees   **YIELD:** 3 loaves

1¼ cups water	⅓ cup evaporated milk
2 Tablespoons instant dry yeast	1 egg
1 Tablespoon sugar	3 Tablespoon canola oil
1½ cups rice pudding	⅓ cup Enrichment Mix
½ cup water	3 cups whole wheat flour
1 Tablespoon sea salt	5-5¼ cups unbleached white flour

In a large bowl or electric mixer bowl, dissolve the yeast in the warm water. Add the sugar. Add 2 cups of white flour. Beat 2 minutes. In the blender, puree the rice pudding, warm water, sea salt, evaporated milk, egg and oil. Add it to the batter. In a small bowl, blend together the whole wheat flour, Enrichment Mix, and remaining white flour. Scrape down the inside of the bowl. When the dough begins to climb the dough hook, turn it out onto a sprinkling of flour. Knead well. Place the dough in an oiled bowl. Turn it to coat all sides of the dough. Cover. Let rise until doubled in bulk.

Punch the dough down. Turn it out on a flat surface and press out the remaining air bubbles. Divide the dough. Let rest 3-4 minutes. Form the loaves. Place in greased pans. Cover and let rise until nearly doubled in bulk. Brush the top of the loaves with oil. Bake. When the loaves are finished, remove them from the pan. Cool on a rack.

RICE PUDDING

Cook the ½ cup of rice according to package instructions. Stir in ¼ cup sugar, ⅓ cup raisins, ¾ cup sweet cream, ½ teaspoon cinnamon, 1 teaspoon vanilla, 2 lightly beaten eggs. Turn into an oiled casserole. Bake 35-40 minutes at 350 degees.

"A spicy spirit and Praise of God always wins the battle."

Edna Lister

 Family Favorites

WINTER SQUASH BREAD

In the fall of the year, when winter squash is economically priced, it's time to stock up. The vegetable is low in calories and it is high in vitamin A. Vitamin A is a stable oil-soluble vitamin, so squash can be steamed and frozen until needed.

OVEN TIME: 30 minutes at 375 degrees   **YIELD:** 2 loaves

1 cup winter squash, cooked & mashed	¼ cup butter, melted
½ cup of pot water from steamed squash	2 eggs
	2 Tablespoons orange zest
¼ cup honey	¼ teaspoon ground ginger
5 teaspoons instant dry yeast	2 teaspoons sea salt
½ cup milk, warm	2 Tablespoons cornmeal
¼ cup sugar, optional	¼ cup pumpkin seeds, chopped
¼ cup orange juice	6½-7 cups unbleached white flour

Steam 1½ cups of winter squash in 1 cup water. Remove from the heat. Strain. Reserve the liquor from the squash. Mash the squash. Cool until warm to the touch. Measure out 1 cup of squash and add 3 Tablespoons honey. Set aside.

In a large bowl or electric mixer bowl, dissolve the yeast in the warm squash water and add the remaining honey, sugar, milk and orange juice. Beat in 2 cups white flour. Beat 2 minutes. Add the butter and the eggs. Beat well. Add the orange zest, squash, pumpkin seeds, ginger and cornmeal. Beat to blend. Scrape down the inside of the bowl. In a separate small bowl, stir together the remaining dry ingredients. Gradually add the mixture to the batter. When the dough leaves the side of the bowl, turn it out onto a sprinkling of flour. Knead the dough until smooth and elastic. Place the dough in an oiled bowl. Turn to coat all sides of the dough with oil. Cover. Let rise until doubled in bulk.

Punch down. Turn out on a flat surface. Press out the remaining air bubbles. Divide the dough into equal portions. Form round loaves. Place them on sprayed baking sheets or in round pans. Let rise to near doubled in bulk. Bake. When the loaves are finished, remove them from the pan. Cool on a rack.

Note: Sweet potatoes or pumpkin can be substituted for the squash.

YEAST CORN BREAD

Note: This creamy colored loaf has a delicate flavor and a light texture. It makes a delicious egg salad or ham salad sandwich for your brown bag lunch. This is a fast rising bread.

OVEN TIME: 30 minutes at 400 degrees   **YIELD:** 2 loaves

2 cups water, or potato water	1 cup warm milk
1 cup cornmeal	4 teaspoons Saf yeast
2 teaspoons sea salt	3 Tablespoons honey
¼ cup butter, melted	2 eggs
3 Tablespoons soy milk powder	3½-4 cups unbleached white flour

Heat the water and sprinkle in the cornmeal. Stir to prevent lumping. Add the sea salt and butter. Remove from the heat. Cool until warm to the touch. In a large bowl or electric mixer bowl, dissolve the yeast in the warm milk. Add the honey. Stir to dissolve. Add 2 cups white flour. Beat 2 minutes. Scrape down the inside of the bowl. Add the cornmeal mixture. Beat to blend. Add the eggs, one at a time. Beat after each addition. Scrape down the inside of the bowl.

Blend the soy milk powder into the remaining flour. Gradually add the mixture to the batter. Scrape down the inside of the bowl. When the dough leaves the side of the bowl, turn it out onto a sprinkling of flour. Knead 6-8 minutes, or until the dough is smooth and elastic. Place the dough in an oiled bowl. Turn to coat all sides. Cover and let rise until doubled in bulk.

Press out the remaining air bubbles. Divide the dough into equal portions. Form the loaves. Place in sprayed, or oiled loaf pans. Let rise until nearly doubled in bulk. Bake on the middle oven rack. When the loaf is finished, remove from the pan. Cool on a rack.

Note: For a different approach to dinner rolls, form slender long rolls and bake in prepared corn stick pans. Sprinkle with cornmeal. Have pans hot before adding the batter.

"Leafing through your troubles leaves smudges
on the pages of your mind."
Ferne Chapman

 Family Favorites

INDEX

INDEX

Please send me ☐ **copies of**
Town & Country Creative Breads
at $14.70 each ($19.95 Canadian)
(Shipping & handling included. Washington State residents add $1.01 sales tax.)

WASHINGTON STATE RESIDENTS:
Number of Copies:
(Shipping, handling & Washington
State sales tax of 7.8% included.)
☐ × **$15.71** = ______________

USA RESIDENTS:
Number of Copies:
(Shipping & handling included.)
☐ × **$14.70** = ______________

CANADIAN RESIDENTS:
Number of Copies:
(Shipping & handling included.)
☐ × **$19.95** = ______________

Please send your **CHECK** or **MONEY ORDER** to:

JacLynn Publishing *2315 - 10 North Pearl Street #243*
Tacoma, Washington 98406

PLEASE DO NOT SEND CASH

Name _________________________________

Address _______________________________

City ___________________________ **State** ___________________

Zip ___________________

BIRTHDAYS ★ WEDDINGS ★ SHOWERS ★ THANK YOUS ★ CHRISTMAS ★ HOUSE WARMINGS

Would you like to give *Town & Country Creative Breads* as a gift?

Simply fill out this Certificate, attach it to the order form and send it along with your **CHECK** or **MONEY ORDER** to:

JacLynn Publishing

2315 - 10 North Pearl St. #243
Tacoma, Washington 98406

PLEASE DO NOT SEND CASH

Gift Recipient

Name _______________________________

Address ____________________________
____
____
____

THE FRED SCHMIDT THRESHING RIG

Excerpt from Pettibone, North Dakota History.